WATERFORD HARBOUR

This book is dedicated to my mother Mary Doherty, née Moran, for her unconditional love and ever-present smile and optimism.

And to the memory of my younger sister Eileen, who died in January of this year. Wife, Mother and a wonderful friend who shared my passion for the sea.

WATERFORD HARBOUR

TIDES AND TALES

ANDREW DOHERTY

Front cover images:
Top: The construction of Dunmore East pier (National Library of Ireland).
Bottom: The dredger Portlairge *(Courtesy of Jonathan Allen).*

Back cover: PS Ida *at Cheekpoint quay (National Library of Ireland).*

First published 2020

The History Press
97 St George's Place, Cheltenham,
Gloucestershire, GL50 3QB
www.thehistorypress.co.uk

British Library Cataloguing in Publication Data.
A catalogue record for this book is available from the British Library.

ISBN 978 0 7509 9368 5

Typesetting and origination by The History Press
Printed in Great Britain by TJ Books Limited, Padstow, Cornwall

CONTENTS

ABOUT THE AUTHOR

Andrew Doherty was born in 1965 in the village of Cheekpoint, Co. Waterford. He followed his family into the tough traditional commercial fishing way of life for fifteen years of his adult life. On the birth of his first child and the  decline of fishing opportunities he worked in local industry before taking up his present career as a community worker. He is involved as a volunteer in village affairs and is passionate about local history and preserving, if not reviving, the traditions of his fishing community.

He has written since his teens and in 2014 commenced a regular blog on the maritime and fishing traditions of the three sister rivers of the Barrow, Nore and Suir, and the harbour of Waterford. His first book, *Before the Tide Went Out*, was published in 2017. A memoir, it examined the culture, identity and practices within the fishing community of his home village and the wider harbour. He has contributed to numerous newspaper articles, heritage publications, radio and TV programmes.

He posts regularly on Facebook and Twitter and blogs at www.tidesandtales.ie

ACKNOWLEDGEMENTS

I have many people to thank for the contents of this book. The majority are named in the pages and I'll let that be a testament to them and my debt to them for their kindness.

A book such as this is not much without pictures. So, I would like to thank Andy Kelly and Brendan Grogan helped me in several ways, particularly with images and technical advice, and I also want to acknowledge the assistance of John Flynn. Thanks to Jonathan Allen for allowing use of his image of the Portlairge, and John O'Connor for the image of the Spit Light.

My good friend Damien McLellan has been a sounding board for many of my ventures and helped in the drafting of this book. I need to thank Carmel Golding and my wife Deena for suggesting edits and giving so freely of their time.

I want to thank Mark Minihan, who was supportive when it was required, and Frank Ronan of Port of Waterford.

I'm indebted to Michael Coady of Carrick on Suir for his advice on the title and the blurb for this book.

Charley McCarthy helped me with specific details on the construction of the Spit/Spider Light, and Myles Courtney gave me some vital information on my quarantine story. I'm indebted to them both.

Hours of research have gone into these stories, much of it on the road. I have a lot to be thankful to Sean Heffernan for, who has kept my car up to the task.

Thanks to Richard Daly, a primary teacher with a love of history and culture who helped enormously with my introduction, and to Jacqui De Suin, who advised on my Irish.

Tides and Tales blog is produced with the support of so many it is hard to list them, but for continuous support I need to acknowledge James Doherty, Frank Murphy, Tomás Sullivan, William Doherty, Maurice Power, Michael Farrell, John O'Sullivan, David Carroll, Paul O'Farrell, Eddie Fardy, Pat O'Gorman and Brian Forristal.

INTRODUCTION

This book originated on the river, as I drifted for salmon with the men of my village, and in the homes of so many seafarers, fishermen and their families.

I was born in Cheekpoint, 7 miles downriver from Waterford City at a point where the Rivers Suir, Barrow and Nore meet. The three rivers then flow as one to create Waterford harbour, entering the Atlantic at Hook Head in Wexford and Dunmore East in Waterford.

My childhood in the 1970s was spent in the company of seafarers and fishermen, listening to their stories, spending time in boats and dreaming of one day following in their wake. When I finally left school in 1983, seafaring was a dying trade, at least to a young apprentice looking to start on the bottom rung of the sailor's career ladder, the ordinary seaman. So I opted instead to go to fish.

I fished full-time from 1983 to 1996 and thereafter part-time to 2006, when the commercial fishery for salmon was closed. In 2014 I set to writing a weekly blog about the heritage of my community and over the years several themes have emerged. My recollections of the commercial fishery were published in a self-published first book *Before the Tide Went Out*. In this book, however, I am reflecting another major theme: old-time stories and yarns that I either thought to be true or wished to be. In the intervening years I have proven many to be based on fact.

The Irish have an old phrase for the passing along of local culture and lore. *Ó Ghlúin go Glúin*, or from knee to knee. In essence it reflects the reality of the past when stories told to one generation whilst sitting on the knee of the forbearer were passed along to succeeding generations. Callers to a home were welcomed, stories and songs were swapped and youngsters were both educated and entertained. So strong was this connection that the Gaelic word for generation is the same as knee.

But the old ways were breaking down when I was a child, the television was sitting in the corner of most homes and, although visitors were welcome, the stories were often those passed on by a presenter from the national broadcaster. But other ways were found, and many was the tale or yarn I heard while drifting for salmon, where the only distractions were the splash of a fish or an obstacle in the boat's path.

The greatest source of my stories has been my father, Bob Doherty: sailor, fisherman, factory worker, gardener and raconteur extraordinaire. But my father's ability to tell a story has sometimes led to questions about their credibility. For example, his tall tales were legion. Pat Murphy, a friend of his who worked with him at the Paper Mills factory in Waterford in the 1970s, recently recalled one such account.

Although we never had a car, Pat did, and as they shared the same shift, he brought my father to work. One very frosty morning Pat drove up out of the village and stopped at the collection point for my father near our home in the Mount Avenue. There was no sign of my father, so Pat continued on to work on his own. A few weeks later Pat was in the canteen in work and thought he'd blackguard (tease) my father and so

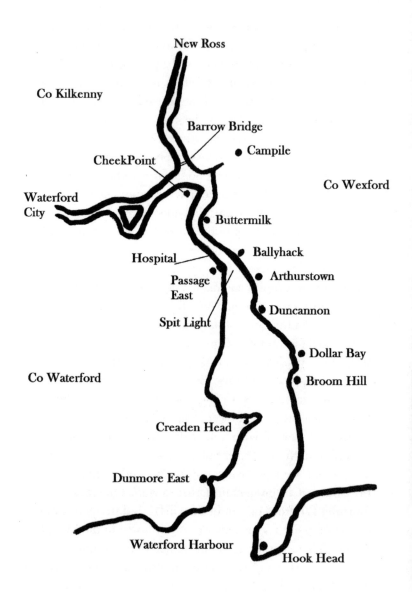

he mentioned to some of his colleagues about Bob sleeping in some weeks previous and turning up late for work.

My father came straight over to the group sitting around the table and made answer:'Well now mates, Pat Murphy don't believe it, but I have since rectified the problem. I was out on the road one day not long after the incident and I met a man and we fell to talking. I mentioned how on frosty nights the clock doesn't work so well. Well the man was an engineer and he was very interested and insisted on seeing it, and after carefully examining it, told me it was a tropical clock. Christ I said, I bought it when sailing overseas in Egypt, but the chap never mentioned that. A few days later a lagging jacket arrived by post from the engineer, and do ye know what? – it hasn't lost a second since.'

According to Pat, each of the men looked from one to the other and then to him. But my father wasn't done yet. 'And I'll tell ye now mates, I haven't been late for Pat Murphy since.'

And all Pat could do was agree, he hadn't. Years after being made redundant following a lock-out at their factory, Pat would still meet his ex-work colleagues and they all wanted to know if Bob Doherty's tropical clock was still keeping time.

So my father had a bit of a reputation when it came to stories, but over the years I have found more than a grain of truth in many of them, as indeed I have found similar in much that I was told as a child. There are no stories of oriental clocks here, but who knows, maybe there will be in the future!

What you can expect are accounts of a life left behind, when the local rivers were chock-a-block full of sailing ships and steam boats, carrying freight to and from the country, crewed by men who knew the hardships of life, and supported or policed by a myriad of other work roles.

1

THE PRESS GANG MENACE

We were drift netting for salmon in a small open punt in the River Suir when I first heard about the press gang menace that troubled the homes and the ships at anchor in the waters around Cheekpoint and Waterford harbour. The story was introduced, like so many others by my father, in a natural yet dramatic way. We were drifting on the ebb tide at night, off Ryan's shore, between Cheekpoint and Passage East on the Waterford side of the river, when we heard a boat rowing towards us. 'If this was the Napoleonic wars I'd have had to throw you over the side for your safety,' he stated flatly. I didn't get a chance to find out why, as Maurice Doherty and Jimmy O'Dea came alongside for a chat before rowing off again to set nets in on the Point Light (a local place name for a river navigation light that marked a stone outcropping). After they left I was keen to clarify how throwing me overboard was good for my health, something I had dwelt on while the three men chatted about matters fish.

The press gangs were Royal Navy sailors who impressed men into the Navy. To impress was basically a form of kidnapping; men were attacked and forcefully taken to make up the numbers in Royal Navy ships. Impressment had operated from the thirteenth century and was most common in times of war. It operated with official sanction up to the early nineteenth century. The press gangs' preference was for young fit men with knowledge of the sea, and as a consequence they became a scourge of Waterford city and the villages throughout the harbour. Merchant ships at anchor were a favoured target. Coming ashore had complications for the press gang, as locals were quick to react and riots were not uncommon in response. But all that information was to come at a later date. On the night my father simply shared a yarn.

'Did I ever tell ya about the man that used to sit in McAlpins Suir Inn and mutter to himself about going with the press gang?' I immediately perked up in anticipation and, not waiting for an answer, he continued with the story:

There was a group of sailors, fishermen and other locals drinking in the bar many years back. Suddenly a cry went up in the village and while many turned to look, there was a man named Walsh with quick wits that turned on his heels and ran to the back door of the pub. As Walsh went through it, he heard the crashing and banging behind him as the press gang rushed the pub's front door. He skipped over a ditch and ran.

Approaching a house, he spotted an open window and dived through it, only to land into the lap of a sleeping lady. On awaking, her first impulse was to scream. At this stage the village was in uproar, some of the press gang crew were going door to door seeking recruits and the women of the village were out shouting abuse and flinging stones in their direction.

At that stage all the men were either captured, in hiding or running towards the top of the local hill, the Minaun. While Walsh pleaded with the lady to be quiet, her father heard her screams and burst in. Now he had been trying to marry his daughter off for some time, and he measured the situation in a heartbeat. Walsh received a chilling ultimatum: the press gang or his daughter's hand. Thereafter Walsh, having had one too many in the pub, could be heard to groan from the bar counter, 'should've went with the press gang'.

The practice of impressment is old, being mentioned in the Magna Carta. It was more common in times of war as competing interests vied for crew. During the Napoleonic wars it became widespread when the navy was stretched and simply didn't have enough men to operate their ships. Apparently the practice had initially started in London but over time and as the needs for crew grew, so did its scope. Waterford was only one of many areas favoured by them, given the quantity of trade, and particularly, it seems, the Newfoundland cod fishery. Crews for the fishery were drawn from farms, villages and towns across the South-East and they flocked to the harbour area to join ships for the cod fishing season on the Grand Banks. These were young, healthy and energetic, and in many ways perfect for the crew-hungry press gangers.

The press gangs had a number of strategies for engaging sailors. These included going ashore to take men from quays, pubs or homes, raiding ships at anchor in harbours or attacking ships on the high seas.

This extract from Waterford of 1777 gives a good example of the practice of going ashore:

The press for seamen still continues here, to the great injury of the trade of this city and the fishery of Newfoundland; several have been picked up lately. Last Wednesday evening the press gang was very roughly treated on the quay, in consequence of their endeavouring to press a man who frequents the fishery of Newfoundland: he (assisted by some female auxiliaries) defended himself with a stick against the attack of the gang, armed with swords, and not withstanding their utmost efforts he got off. By this time a party of resolute fellows assembled, and by pelting of stones soon made the gang disappear. But their resentment did not stop here, for they done considerable damage to the house of Mr Shanahan, publican, on the Quay, where the press gang rendezvous; and had not a party of the army been ordered out to disperse them and prevent further mischief it is probable some fatal consequences would have happened.[1]

This account also highlights a major disadvantage of a shore-side press – the reaction of the local citizenry.

So if a shore-side press was injurious to the press gang's health, a relatively safer approach was to board vessels at anchor, under cover of darkness. At Cheekpoint, on what was described as a 'dark and tempestuous' night in October 1779, HMS *Licorne* was at anchor and in need of extra men to supplement her crew. Conditions were considered favourable to a stealth attack and so under the command of Lieutenant Rudsdale a party set off in the ship's pinnace (a small tender/rowing boat). They immediately drew alongside a local fishing punt and, in case the men aboard reported the navy's activities, they 'pressed the lot'. Rudsdale returned to his vessel to drop off his captives and set off again towards

Passage and Ballyhack. There they boarded the anchored brig *Triton* and, finding the crew asleep, pressed as many crew as he could fit in the pinnace. Dropping them back to the *Licorne*, he again returned to the *Triton*, but this time the press gangers were confronted by a barrage of spikes, hatchets and crowbars. He withdrew, and the piece goes on to say that, the racket having raised the harbour villages, he was forced to return to his ship. Rudsdale was apparently satisfied with his night's work; he had secured a score of men (twenty) to add to his vessel's crew.[2]

The other approach was to attack ships at sea, and in many cases merchant men were stripped of their capable crew and very often such men were swapped with either injured or incapable sailors, deemed unfit for the navy. Even in circumstances where armed naval vessels were employed, however, successful outcomes were not guaranteed. For example, an unnamed Newfoundland vessel sailing to Waterford on 5 November 1770 was challenged by a 'press boat' off Cork harbour. The crew and passengers were up for a fight, however, and following an exchange of gunfire the press boat thought it best to sheer off. Five aboard the Newfoundlander were wounded and it put in to Youghal, where one of the injured died. Meanwhile, the press boat put in to Dungarvan, where her wounded crew received treatment.[3]

Several other accounts of the press gangs have come to my attention, including a shore-based captain who organised the impressment of sailors from an office at Passage East, a press gang that went ashore in Waterford city – resulting in 140 men pressed on the quay – and the landing of another press gang on the Hook peninsula and their working along the coast to Duncannon.

The press gang diminished after the Napoleonic wars. A peacetime navy required fewer sailors, but naval reforms and improved pay helped encourage voluntary recruitment. Social reformers also helped in fighting the hated practice by pamphleteering, newspaper articles and rallies. The next great naval dispute against Russia in the Crimea in 1853 is said to be the first in which impressed sailors did not serve.

All those insights had yet to come, however. Sitting on the thwart of the punt that night, drifting away on the tide, I was for a few short moments transported away from under the cold star-flecked sky. Tiredness was momentarily forgotten and I laughed into the night, careful however not to be too loud. Noise spooked the salmon we sought and I knew from childhood not to disturb the fish. More importantly, however, I also felt a little closer to my father.

For all I've learned since though, I'm still unsure if Walsh and the wife that was 'pressed' on him is true or not!

2

MYSTERIOUS
BUTTERMILK CASTLE

In the wide-ranging mud flats, inlets, headlands and bays that make up the harbour it would come as no surprise to know that we have a multitude of place names and marks that signify where you are at any particular time. Such names were vitally important in the past to fishermen, denoting as they did as precise a position as any modern satellite aid. Some of these were functional, some literal and others were very confusing, particularly to a child. One that springs to mind in this latter category was Buttermilk Castle, more commonly called by the fishermen 'the Castle'.

The castle was a formidable lump of rock with a crown of pine trees on the river above Ballyhack in Co. Wexford. An associated fishing weir for catching salmon shared the same name. The rock jutted resolutely into the river, like a brooding citadel, but when I sought further information my youthful questions were usually brushed aside. We drifted close by when fishing, but that didn't answer any questions either – the building that gave the place its name had crumbled into the cliff, and was swallowed up by an undergrowth of briar, fern and gorse.

My father did share one story that appealed to my youthful imagination and it went something like this. The Old IRA[4] had an active unit operating in South West Wexford and the unit leader was from the Duncannon area. They were constantly on the move, seeking safe houses. One evening they found themselves camped at Buttermilk. Informers were often a problem and intelligence was leaked as to their whereabouts. A Royal Navy gunboat was summoned and was a regular visitor in the harbour. The captain had fallen fond of a local girl on many of his trips ashore, but awkwardly enough the object of his desire was a sister of the leader of the IRA active service unit.

When the location of the hideout of the unit was received, the gunboat was dispatched with orders to launch an attack. According to my father, in an attempt to keep the girl sweet, rather than attack the castle directly the captain decided to steam up past the spot, and made a great show of turning and readying his guns. By the time they commenced firing the unit was already safely over the hill and heading towards Ballyhack. The only damage they did was to weaken the structure of the castle itself.

My first proper view of what the castle looked like came when visiting a wonderful maritime museum, which was located at Duncannon Fort, back in the 1990s. Alas no more now, the museum had a photograph of the Castle, taken by the noted Waterford photographer A.H. Poole in the late nineteenth century. It depicted the familiar square-shaped Norman tower house overlooking the river.

But where one question is answered, others very often arise. And so it was with Buttermilk. Why a castle in such an out of the way spot? And what was its purpose? Locally the accepted wisdom stated it was part of the elaborate farm and business of the Cistercian Abbey at Dunbrody, Campile, Co. Wexford. The monks constructed it as a protection and comfort for their fishing monks, who were working the associated weir, and at least two others in the harbour. Recently I've heard it described as a strategic location with which to exploit the economic opportunities presented by Waterford harbour.

Now economic potential suggests to me something other than fishing a weir, or managing butter transport. That and the fact that it's an elaborate build just to keep the rain off fishermen. Tower houses were usually built for defence. The location would not protect it much from the land, but would certainly be formidable from the river. Was it more of a secure location, a place where business could be transacted and valuables stored?

It's undoubtedly true that the weirs were a commercial success in the harbour, and were a vital element in the trade from the area to the Continent.[5] Rental to Dunbrody of three fishing weirs was equal in value to the rental of half a ploughland at 48s 4d[6], underlining their value in the 1400s.

Of course, foreign fishing fleets were also working the harbour and off the coast. Such fleets needed secure landing places to dry or salt their catch. Is it possible that it was an administrative centre for such activities? The monks certainly would have had the contacts. I also heard it described as a toll house, and indeed a water gate. I find the notion of a toll house fascinating. In modern times, we might think Buttermilk is a bit out of the way, but in medieval times some of the maps depicting the harbour show the shipping channel avoiding Carters Patch on the Waterford side, by swinging over towards Wexford and close by the castle.[7]

Another feature of the place was a safe anchorage. Ships then, as now, would have sought out such places whilst waiting for a cargo or a position in port. Even now the site is still highly regarded as a safe anchorage, albeit for yachts and pleasure boats.

I've never heard anyone speculate as to why a tower built to protect weirs would be called after a dairy by-product. According to my grandmother, the name of the castle came from the fact that it was used as a transport point between Dunbrody and Faithlegg. She said that butter was made on the site from milk gathered from the Waterford side of the harbour on a Faithlegg farm under their control. Personally I would see it as making more sense that it was used as a point from which dairy products were exported. Whatever the truth of it, the reality is that over millennia the chances are that Buttermilk Castle served several purposes, some of which we may never realise. Indeed, Billy Colfer speculated that the promontory was once known by a Norse name, Skeroirke, or rock.[8] How many other names may it have had down the generations?

The strangest part of my story is that apparently my grandmother was the only witness to the collapse of the castle. The story goes that on a very cold frosty morning in the 1930s she was throwing the bucket of slops up on the ditch across the road from the house. As the slops hit the ditch, a billow of steam rose up against the cold frosty air, and in that exact instant she saw a billow of dust rising up from Buttermilk, and moments later the sound of falling masonry.

Today, if you visit the site by water you will see the foundation and the stone that made up the base of the castle. If you ever get the opportunity to step in on it, you will appreciate the strategic view it afforded. Whatever purposes it served from the time of the Cistercians, or indeed before them, we will probably never know.

3

CHEEKPOINT MAIL PACKET STATION

Being immersed in a fishing and seafaring community, you get accustomed to flow and ebb, comings and goings. Ships, people and trends come and go, perhaps not as frequently as the tides, but with the same inevitability. One era that came and went, and which was little more than a folk memory as a child, was the time of the mail packets running from Cheekpoint.

The story of the packets was aided, however, by three very distinctive, tangible relics. The first was the main quay, which although refurbished in the late nineteenth century was of a similar shape and design to what had been in position previously. The second was a four-storey Georgian building of brick and stone on the west side of the village that was described as the packet or coaching inn. The other was more of a curiosity; a milestone located on the approach to the village that gave the distance to the city and the quay.

Tales were told of fast sailing vessels loading or unloading beside the quay. Images came to mind of carriages trundling through the village collecting or depositing passengers and postal sacks. Or teams of horses dragging cargo into and out of the village and a general hustle and bustle associated with a busy port. There were accounts of related industries that accompanied the packets, cotton and linen works, brickmaking and the remains of lime kilns to the east of the village.

The milestones had once run the length of the road to Waterford, but many were removed for fear of a German invasion during the Second World War. Indeed, the one at Cheekpoint had also been knocked down at that time, but had been reinstated by workmen who found it when building the nearby council houses in the Mount Avenue in the 1960s.

In my childhood the hotel was derelict. Its only saving grace to me, with its shattered windows and crumbling brickwork, was an old orchard at the back yielding some very tasty apples. According to the records, it opened in 1793 as a coaching inn under a manager named Sly, a name hardly inspiring confidence or trust. A later manager, William Jackson, 'rose early, went down to the pier, threw himself in the river and was drowned'. It was said locally as he left that morning he'd put on a heavy overcoat and, as he walked to the river, stuffed his pockets with stones that he picked off the road as he went. In 1808 James Howley was running the hotel and the venture was expanding. He was overseeing the erection of new stables for as many as ten horses. I have read three accounts or reviews of those who stayed at the hotel – none of them were very positive and one is blunt and to the point: 'It was dark before we reached Cheek Point – where there is a large dirty inn – for the reception of Packet Passengers.' [9]

The origins of the Cheekpoint packet date to the late eighteenth century, when the mails to and from the Waterford area were an ad-hoc affair. A great account can be gleamed from the visit of Arthur Young to the region in 1776, indeed it is arguable that he would not have stayed in the area but for the precarious nature of the packets at the time. Young was travelling the country on an agricultural tour and was to embark on a packet ship at Passage for a return to England.[10] The vessel's captain made all manner of excuses not to sail though, and realising the delay was to build up a passenger manifest, the traveller decided to invite himself to stay with the local landlord.

At the time the packet boats had evolved to carry packages of business, government and domestic mail, passengers and freight transportation between European countries and their colonies. However, the service out of Waterford, and based at Passage East, was a privately run operation, carrying post, but depending also on passengers and freight to generate income. The official postal route between London and Ireland was via Holyhead to Dublin.

Pressure had been building on the postal service, however, from business interests in the Bristol and Waterford area for some time. Travel was unpredictable to say the least on the existing private service, as Arthur Young found to his cost. The official channel via Dublin was slow when road transport between Dublin and the cities and towns of Munster was factored in. Further leverage in the campaign for a regular service appears to have been the need for up-to-date intelligence on the French fleet during the Napoleonic wars, as indicated in this excerpt from a letter of the time appealing for the service: '… a few hours in the arrival of a dispatch might be the means of taking or destroying a fleet of the Enemy or saving our own …'[11]

By 1786 the Post Office began working to make a second route to Ireland a reality, and the Cheekpoint Packet officially commenced on 5 April 1787 with one ship and one sailing a week under the management of a Welsh Quaker named Thomas Owen. The service would cater for travellers from thirty-eight towns in the southern region, all of whom routed through Waterford and hence Cheekpoint. It must have been an early success because by June of that year the packet had extended to five trips a week and by August five ships were running six days per week, every day but Saturday.[12]

In 1790 Thomas Owen was given a seven-year contract to the value of £1,200 per annum to run the service. He lost this to Samuel Newport in 1793[13], but his name continued to be associated with the service, so I can only speculate that Owen continued to manage it on Newport's behalf.

An amazing record was said to be set during this time. The distance between Cheekpoint and Milford Haven was 85 miles. It was claimed to have been covered on one occasion in eight hours, the average said to have been something between nine and fifteen hours. The ships used were cutters of about 80–90 tons and known for their speed, an important consideration as they had to outrun French privateers. Some of the ships running on the service in 1788 were *Carteret*, *Walsingham*, *Ponsonby*, *Clifden* and the *Tyrone*.[14]

In 1810 plans were announced to develop a new harbour at Dunmore, and with the death of Thomas Owen in 1813 the packet moved, initially to Passage East and eventually to Dunmore East in 1818. The East was added to Dunmore at that time to avoid confusion with another Dunmore in Galway for postage purposes. The mails continued to arrive and depart until 1835. But with the coming of steam power and the ability to bend the winds and tides to the will of the ships, the packet moved to Waterford city, where it operated until 1850. (The Great Western Railway Co. would later fulfil the postal requirements.)

The criticism against using the harbour at Cheekpoint was its distance from the harbour mouth. Sailing ships had to depend on tides and wind to aid their journey up river. However, steam power was already on the way, and it's interesting to note that as early as 1824, they were employed on the Milford–Dunmore East route.[15]

Despite the bad hotel reviews, Howley followed the service to Passage East and set up as manager of a hotel there to accommodate packet users. His family later emigrated to Newfoundland and a descendant recently visited the area and called at my home in the company of William Doherty to discuss the family connections in the area. The hotel at Cheekpoint was refurbished in the 1990s and is now a family home. The quay remains, but could do with refurbishment. Meanwhile, the writing on the milestone fades further with each passing year.

I often wondered, what if steam-powered vessels had been introduced a decade earlier on the route? Would the village I grew up in have been a much different place, in ways I probably can never truly imagine? I will never know.

4

RIVER PADDLE
STEAMER SERVICE

Christy Doherty was one of the old-school fishermen who I met regularly as a child. A quiet, inoffensive man, he liked nothing better than to light a cigarette, take his ease against an upturned boat and fall to storytelling. He had a great knowledge of the river and fishing, and when asked about the weather would always look to the sky and take in his surroundings before forecasting the day to come. When I was a child he always addressed me as 'u sir', which was a way the older men had of greeting, and probably spared them having to remember all the names. One of the lasting memories I have of him is his accounts of the paddle steamers calling to Cheekpoint quay, picking up passengers and heading down to Dunmore East for a regatta, or Duncannon for a day on the beach.

Now as a child such tales made me wary: I was both fascinated and cautious about them. I'd imagine that most of us growing up in that era were so used to hearing tall stories that it was often impossible to tell when the truth ended and the yarns took over. Evaluating stories was further complicated by the way the older guys tended to collude with each other. As you went from one to the other, they could often embellish a yarn rather than correct it. Amateurs might be caught out with a wink or a slight grin, but for the master story tellers you might search their face in vain for even the slightest hint that they were 'rising you'. So in time to come I was fascinated to learn the truth of the river service, the ships that travelled it and the vibrancy that was the rivers in an era that seems to me now a golden age.

The regular river service originated with the Waterford Steam Navigation Company, which was formed in 1836 to provide cross-channel steamship services. In 1837 a river service was initiated, providing links between the city and both New Ross and Duncannon. The fundamental function of the services seems to have been the supply of foodstuffs to both the city of Waterford and for export, and cattle, sheep, pigs, fowl and horses were the backbone of the cargo. Two new paddle steamers were constructed to ply the routes. The *Shamrock* (135 tons) was built in 1836 in Glasgow; the *Duncannon* (200 tons) was launched in the John Laird yard of Birkenhead in 1837.[16]

An advert from a contemporary newspaper gives a sense of the schedule and price:

> *Shamrock* leaves Ross 8.45 a.m. arriving at 10 a.m..
> Returns from Waterford at 3 p.m.. Except Sundays
> Fare: Cabin 2 Shillings. Deck 1 Shilling 3 pence.

> *Duncannon* arrives at 9.15 a.m. every morning
> Leaves Waterford for Ballyhack and Duncannon daily at
> 4 p.m.. 3 p.m. in winter.
> Fares: Cabin 1 Shilling. Deck 6 pence

The PS *Duncannon* ran until 1861, and when she needed a break for repairs a relief steamer, the PS *Taff* (1844 – 90 tons) was used. She was replaced by the PS *Tintern* (1861, 147 tons), which operated up until the 1870s and was subsequently replaced by the PS *Vandeleur (*151 tons). The *Tintern* was then used as a relief vessel. The *Vandeleur* was built in the Neptune iron works of Waterford (Park Road) in 1866 for the Shannon estuary, where she served until her return to Waterford. She was originally constructed as a partner vessel to the PS *Rosa (*1863, 148 tons), a ship that was also to feature on the river service of Waterford. One other ship I am aware of was the *Repealer*. She sailed the Waterford–New Ross route for at least a season in 1842, but she seems to have been a short-lived competitor rather than a relief boat.

The following year, 1867, the Neptune turned out another paddle steamer that went onto the New Ross route, the PS *Ida* (172 tons). It appears that the *Ida* replaced the *Shamrock*, but another ship mentioned on the route was the PS *Maid of Erin* (1839, 99 tons)[17]. The *Ida* was launched by Neptune on Friday, 27 September 1867 and was described at the time as, 'A very handsome little paddle steamer … of unusual size (149 ft x 19ft x 9ft) and beauty … intended to ply between this city (Waterford) and (New) Ross.'

The *Ida* made her maiden voyage from Waterford on Friday, 31 January 1868 accompanied by the PS *Shamrock*, making it in one hour ten minutes. Both vessels received a terrific reception when they reached the New Ross quays despite dreadful weather. *Ida* would be a constant sight on the Suir and Barrow for the next thirty-seven years. The steamers transported freight, fish, agriculture produce and passengers. The *Ida* departed New Ross at 8.15 a.m. each morning (Monday to Saturday), making stops as required at quaysides along the way. They would make prearranged stops at places such as Pilltown and Great Island in Co. Wexford, and the ferry at Ballinlaw, Co. Kilkenny. The Duncannon steamer generally called to Ballyhack, Passage East and Cheekpoint; apparently it was all down to whether there were passengers or freight requiring transport.

Here's a fascinating contemporary account of the *Ida* connecting with the Ballinlaw ferry that ran between Co. Kilkenny and Great Island in Co. Wexford:

> the most exciting experience of all was at Ballinlaw, when the ponderous ferry-boat with passengers and farm produce from the Great Island made contact with the Ida as she lay to midstream. To get the passengers safely aboard by means of a companion ladder involved considerable risk in rough weather. But the Ballinlaw boatmen knew their job, and no accident occurred in living memory.[18]

Once in Waterford, the *Ida* and her sister ship the PS *Vandeleur* could be assigned to various tasks in the port; towage, maintenance works, and indeed salvage and rescue missions. I'd imagine there was many a fisherman or boatman could thank these ships for a tow into town or up the Ross River against the tides, providing them with a welcome respite to working the oars and rowing the long distances that was their daily grind.

The weekday services ran Monday to Saturday but Sundays in summer months were used for special event trips. Bill Irish quotes one such account:

> I have very pleasant memories of the shilling trips return every Sunday by steamer from Waterford to Dunmore East and the splendid tea for eight pence at Galgeys or Shipseys

Hotel at Dunmore. These trips were the best value that has ever been offered to Waterford residents. The boats the Ida and Vandeleur left about mid-day or 3pm on alternate Sundays. We had three hours in Dunmore and reached Waterford at 10pm.

As lovely as it sounds, it would appear to be very costly for ordinary folk.

Another account I have comes via Bill Irish from an interview with Captain Farrell of one such trip on the *Ida* to Duncannon when he was a boy. 'A man named Friday, with one eye, played a melodeon box on the way up and down the river. The hat was then put around for a collection. The *Ida* stopped in Duncannon for about one hour to allow people to "stretch their legs". Along with the captain, was a first mate, two men to handle ropes, two engineers and two firemen.'

There were many episodes associated with the river service that I have come across, but for sheer madness the following account takes the biscuit. On Saturday evening, 23 July 1870, the *Ida* departed her normal berth at the hulk (I presume based on the events mentioned that this was the Duncannon Hulk, which was located close to where the present large blue crane is situated on Waterford's quays) on the quay at 4 p.m. She proceeded down the Suir.

Opposite the Mall, a drunken passenger jumped on to the railings and hurled himself into the river. The *Ida* immediately stopped her engines and the crew tried to effect a rescue. The gentleman was struggling in the water, fully clothed and with his boots on. However, he didn't seem minded to accept the crew's help.

The clerk of the Waterford Petty Sessions, Mr P.F. Hanrahan, was rowing by in a small boat and came close to the man, offering him an oar. He was met with abuse and, turning on his back, the 'drowning man' proceeded to kick water and practically overturn Hanrahan's craft. A boatman in a prong met a similar fate.

A daring dock worker named Kelly had also decided to help, and he stripped on the quay and dived into the river, but on swimming towards the victim he got nothing but abuse. Kelly was picked up by the prong and both men managed to overpower and haul the villain aboard. Rather than appreciation, the man reacted with fists, and in the melee that ensued Kelly knocked him out. His companion hastily rowed ashore, where the rescued man was arrested on the spot by awaiting constabulary.

Meanwhile, another rescue was required. A considerable crowd had assembled quayside and in an effort to get a better vantage of the incident, some rushed aboard the ship *Malakoff,* moored alongside the quay. Proceeding to the bridge, they leaned out to view the scene, pressing against some netting designed to provide security. However, it was not capable of taking the weight that was now placed on it. The netting ripped and ten spectators ended up in the Suir fighting for their lives! All were successfully rescued by a fleet of small boats that were gathered at the scene.

The instigator of the drama was whisked off by the police. The newspaper correspondent earnestly concludes his piece in the hope that that the miscreant will face the full force of the law at the next court session, something assured if Mr Hanrahan had any part in it surely.[19]

So many dramas, so many journeys and so many memories. The end of the river operation came with the undermining of the freight and passenger service by the railways. The *Ida* last sailed on her route in the first week of July 1905, steaming down the Barrow towards Waterford with her boats, landing hulk and other paraphernalia in tow. Her company flag flew at half-mast. Her final journey from Waterford took her to Bristol, where apparently she was broken up at Clevedon Pill in 1908 after thirty-seven years of loyal service.

Due to the distance of South West Wexford from the nearest railway head at Campile, Ballycullane or Wellington Bridge, a service continued between Duncannon and Waterford city until 1917. The *Vandeleur* was retired, but a replacement, the SS *Duncannon,* maintained the route until she too was taken off, apparently requisitioned for war duties. Despite appeals from the locality, the service was not reinstated.

Hearing those stories as a child gave me a yearning to take a similar voyage and I was interested to see that when researching the accounts of the river steamers, there were numerous letters and articles to the local papers for several decades after they last sailed. It suggested to me a deep love and regard for these boats and those who ran them.

I'm indebted to the work of the late Bill Irish for much of the detail in this piece. Bill was an early encourager of my research.

A view out of the harbour with Passage East on the right, Ballyhack on the left. A sketch by Thomas Phillips circa 1685 for a survey of required defence recommendations for securing the Kingdom of Ireland against attack or invasion. Thomas Phillips's Irish survey was submitted by Lord Dartmouth to the Lord Lieutenant of Ireland, James Butler, 1st Duke of Ormond. The Lord Lieutenant submitted the survey to the Privy Council in 1685, but the proposals were not implemented. (National Library of Ireland)

The construction of Dunmore East pier. A print by William Henry Bartlett from an engraving by T. Dixon. Catalogue of Irish topographical prints and original drawings, Rosalind M. Elmes. New edition revised and enlarged by Michael Hewson. Dublin: Malton Press for the National Library of Ireland Society, 1975. p. 91. (National Library of Ireland)

Buttermilk Castle, from an original by A.H. Poole of Waterford. Note the pleasure craft in the foreground. (Author's Collection)

PS *Ida* underway with a large crowd aboard, presumably for a special event trip given the numbers and the decorative flags flying from her mast. Note the company flag atop. (A.H. Poole originally, Author's Collection)

PS *Ida* at Cheekpoint quay before the Barrow Bridge commenced. Note poles along quay for spreeting (hanging to dry) salmon fishing nets and a pilot house in bottom left where pilots could rest and await ships. (National Library of Ireland)

The construction commences on the Barrow Railway Viaduct. Photo dated 21 April 1903 taken from Great Island, Co. Wexford, with a steam yacht in the foreground. (Courtesy of Royal Commission on the Ancient & Historic Monuments of Scotland)

The completed bridge circa 1930. This photograph was actually taken from Great Island, Co. Wexford, looking across the River Barrow towards Co. Kilkenny. (Courtesy of Waterford County Museum)

5

Dollar Bay Pirates

Of all the stories that I heard from my father while fishing there was one in particular that stood out as being very fanciful and incredible. It concerned an old sailing ship from centuries before and, as my father put it, 'Four of the crew turned to piracy and cut the throats of their fellow seafarers and passengers and made off with a treasure, part of which they buried at Cheekpoint.'

I later read an account of the incident in my grandmother's weekly copy of the *Ireland's Own* magazine and my jaw fell open. The story is now freely available on the internet if you care to search for it. There are also many different written accounts,[20] but the version I heard told by my father was as follows.

The sailing ship *Earl of Sandwich* departed in the winter of 1765 from the Canary Islands bound for England. Aboard was a cargo of wine and other general freight, but it was a passenger by the name of Captain George Glass that was most significant to what would unfold. He was a retired privateer (government-licensed pirate), returning to his home country with a small fortune collected from years of adventuring abroad. Travelling with him was his wife and daughter.

The ship was commanded by a Captain Cochrane; a wily and capable seaman. He knew that both he and his crew would be sorely tested in sailing through the Atlantic winter storms. However, he probably had never countenanced, let alone planned to deal with, the trouble coming his way.

Sometime in November the ship arrived off the Waterford coast near to the Hook and it was at this stage that four of the crew turned rogue. My father couldn't say why, but he guessed one, if not all of them, had sailed with Captain Glass before and knew what he was stowing aboard. However they knew, they must have plotted the whole trip, planning for a time that would be ripe for the taking of the ship. The attack was swift and as they slit throats with knives, or ran them through with swords, they tossed the passengers and their shipmates over the side.

Once free of interference, they set to gathering their booty and celebrating their good fortune. Realising that they needed to get away from the ship with their spoils, they launched the ship's tender but the gold they had gathered could scarcely be contained safely aboard. There were also jewels to be carried and a measure of gold ore. They scuttled the sailing ship and pushed off, rowing hard for the nearest landfall, which was on the Hook peninsula at Templetown, Co. Wexford.

They must have had a difficult row in their overloaded boat, but eventually landfall was made. Hauling their boat up on the shore, they hid it along with the treasure before walking to the local inn for food and beer. Apparently the four strangers caused many raised eyebrows when they pushed in the door of the local inn. Foreign sailors were not uncommon, but it was their ability to spend Spanish gold that made the men really stand out.

With suspicions aroused, the men left earlier than they had planned. Returning to their boat, they retrieved both it and the treasure. A decision was taken to bury a sizeable portion to be collected at a later time, and under cover of darkness they departed upriver. Their plan, most probably, was to blend in and cause less suspicion in the port, where hundreds of sailors would be gathered. Later the same day they arrived at New Ross and quickly found an inn to put their heads down, quench their thirst and most likely enjoy some female company.

Although they had damaged the hull of the *Earl of Sandwich*, presuming it would sink to the ocean floor, the ship had actually washed up on the coast of Waterford. The authorities were most perplexed by the ship with no crew. Examinations on board suggested foul play, and officials along the coast went in search of the ship's tender and potential survivors. Word of the four sailors spreading largesse at Templetown reached their ears and a manhunt ensued. Although some say they were captured at New Ross, or others in Dublin, my father said that they fled downriver, heading back to retrieve their treasure and to hopefully catch a ship outward bound.

The authorities chased them down at Fisherstown Bank on the River Barrow (known to this day as Dollar Point) close to Cheekpoint, where they were rescued from a sinking boat, having pushed off from the shore at the sight of the onrushing troops. Apparently they had stashed some of the money on the shore and were disturbed having just retrieved it. Some of the gold went down with the boat, and my father said there was many the beam trawl set on Fisherstown Bank for years after in the hopes of dragging up Spanish coin.

Once captured, the pirates were 'interviewed' and a follow-up search of the beach at Templetown yielded over two hundred bags of gold, which was taken by armed guard to the Custom House on New Ross quay. The event led to the origin of the place name: Dollar Bay! The men might have hoped for leniency having given up the treasure but instead they were sent to trial, found guilty and sentenced to death. They met their fate with the hangman and their bodies were hung at various points around Dublin docks as a warning to other sailors.[21]

The question remained, however, was all the treasure retrieved? My father was adamant that it was not, claiming that for years after, men searched the shoreline between New Ross and the Hook on both sides in the hope that the pirates had hidden more. Stories abounded of coins and other valuables being uncovered where the wreck had washed ashore west of Tramore, too. A story persisted in Cheekpoint of suspicious lights being seen on Ryan's shore, or voices of foreigners carrying up from the shore in the night, at the time of the pirate's journey in their boat of gold! It was considered plausible that the canny pirates had stashed part of their haul in various locations to maximise their chances of retrieving the hoard.

Historically it's known that the local landlord, Cornelius Bolton, a contemporary of the pirates, had dug up vast areas along the local riverbank under the pretext of looking for slate or coal. He had English soldiers employed in the operation and the shafts and pits they dug are still to be seen. Nothing of value was discovered, it was said, and he later went broke.

What I know for certain is that in the late 1990s during a gale, a very large and ancient tree fell on Ryan's Shore below Cheekpoint and my father was one of the first over to inspect it. He had long suspected that gold might be lying under its roots. Alas he told me, when he got there, 'There was nothing to be found, but …,' he said conspiratorially, 'there were other footprints in the clay!'

6

WEIR WARS

The Doherty family had a number of fishing weirs when I was a lad, and I understood the value of them in terms of catching bait in summer months for luring eels into the fishing pots, and foodstuff in winter such as cod, whiting or plaice. Given their importance, I was appalled as a youngster to hear stories of an attack on them. The story, which was the same no matter who recounted it, told of the day the cot fishermen of Carrick-On-Suir and New Ross descended *en masse* on Cheekpoint and proceeded to cut down the fishing weirs in the river. The cot[22] men were bazzed (a local term for throwing stones or, less menacingly, snowballs) out of it with stone by women and children but great damage was done to the weirs. One cot was overturned, resulting in a man drowning.

In recent years I've heard it described as the weir wars, and indeed as it happens it was like a war, and like many such events there had to be a strong motivating factor to bring the cot men together and to take the law into their own hands.

There were broadly two types of weir in the lower harbour. The most common, and still partially in use, were the head weirs, the origins of which go back at least to the coming of the Normans in the 1170s. These weirs were a large fishing

structure, built in the rivers using timber poles in a v formation, and they harnessed the power of the tidal rivers to catch
fish. As the tide ran, the weir poles funnelled the water into
a narrow chute called the head, from which a net was hung.
Fish were swept into the net and retrieved by fishermen.[23] Fish
had a fighting chance, however – a king's/queen's pass was
enforced, meaning the structures could not block the river
entirely and they were most effective on only very strong tides.
I believe this method of weir was employed exclusively up to
the start of the nineteenth century.

In the first or second decade of the nineteenth century, a
new type of weir was introduced, in general called a Scotch
weir due to its origins. Salmon was the intended catch. The
impetus for this fishing technique was the introduction of a
new preserving technique using ice, which was introduced
from China. Steam power and railways also assisted in speed
of transport. Heretofore, salmon could only be sold in a fresh
state locally. Now they could travel, and the appeal of fresh
salmon led to a growing demand.

Scotch weirs were also made with poles and generally ran
from high water mark to beyond lower water. They were
placed perpendicular to the shore and worked effectively to
block the passage of anything up or down the river. What
it meant was that fish, particularly salmon, which swam
upriver to spawn, were blocked in their natural passage by
these timber structures. Not only did it block their means of
reproduction by preventing them getting to the spawning
grounds, it also reduced the potential catch of all the other
fishermen that operated in the narrower waters upriver.

The Scotch weirs were owned by landlords (it was the
same with the head weirs), who leased out their operation

to local fishermen. However, the effectiveness of these weirs caused severe difficulties for local fishermen along the length of the Barrow, Nore and Suir. Indeed, they were problematic wherever they were found. Newspapers carried many stories of traditional fishermen complaining of their livelihoods being destroyed. However, as the structures were owned and made money for the landlord class, who had control of the courts, the law and the army, then what could ordinary citizens do?

The first mention I have as yet found of trouble was 1828, when the use of the weirs was questioned and their removal mooted. In 1833 a newspaper report stated that, 'Captain Murphy and a detachment of the 70th regiment are now stationed at Passage for the purpose of preventing the peasants from injuring the salmon weirs in the district.'[24] Another detachment of the same regiment was based at Duncannon (further out the harbour on the Wexford side). Tensions were obviously starting to grow.

In 1835 the St Peter's Society was founded in New Ross after the traditional fishers of the three rivers came together to advocate for action.[25] Although the risk to the salmon stocks and the difficulties posed to hundreds of fishing families was clear to many, matters lay unresolved, tensions continued to rise and desperate men were forced to take desperate measures. *The Dublin Penny Journal* of 1836 gives the following account:

> the cotmen assembled to the number of two hundred cots and armed with hatchets, saws, etc., braved the dangers of the sea in their small boats which are generally built of four or five boards. They left Ross in the morning, accomplished

their object and returned on the tide exhausted and fatigued, having performed a voyage of nearly fifty miles. The lovers of cheap salmon welcomed their return with three hearty cheers and made a handsome collection to buy bread and beer to refresh these nautical heroes.[26]

The account I was reared on corresponds with an article from the *Freemans Journal* of 1844.[27] In brief it stated that more than fifty cots appeared off Cheekpoint, carrying two to three men in each armed with hatchets, billhooks, scythes, etc. Seventeen came down the Suir past the city, the remainder being from New Ross. They cut down two weirs on the Wexford shore, initially probably at Great Island; they then crossed over to Cheekpoint and destroyed the weir of a 'poor woman, the widow Walsh, who begged of them, on her knees, not to destroy it; but her entreaties being in vain ... .' Next they visited the Spit at Passage where they were 'cheered by the majority of the Passage folks ...' where another Scotch weir was cut, next to a weir at the Church Point (below Ballyhack in Wexford), and they then returned upriver. However, here things went awry. A man named Meathe (locally Meades dock is still used as a place name by fishermen located between Cheekpoint and Passage East on the Waterford side) successfully protected his weir by displaying a heap of stones to ward off the cots. At the next weir they encountered a fisherman named Doherty (another report gave his first name as Andrew, my forefather), who called some of them by name and so they moved on. When returning to the Ross River (the River Barrow is locally often called the Ross River even today) a man fell overboard and drowned.

The weirs must have been wrecked and rebuilt many times after. At a cursory glance through the newspapers, numerous events, altercations, parliamentary hearings and court cases occurred in subsequent years. One poignant article I read from the height of the famine relates how cots that were employed in removing weirs from the Barrow had been confiscated, leaving their owners with no means of earning an income. It was not until the 1860s that new rules emerged to outlaw the majority of Scotch weirs. In most cases the head weirs were not affected, and even some of the Scotch weirs survived.

A few of the head weirs are still in existence today and are as valuable a piece of Irish heritage as you will get. I suppose their inaccessibility, and perhaps the Irish lack of interest for the sea and its history, works against a greater appreciation and understanding of the structures themselves and their fishing method.

My adult research of the weir wars mark a deeper, if darker understanding of a very difficult era. Just like cheering for the cowboys and booing the Indians in my youthful movie-watching days, I'm now less inclined to cheer the bazzing of the cot men, and have a greater appreciation of their struggles in providing for their families. That said, however, I'm sure that had I been there I'd have picked up them stones.

7

LOSS OF THE
ALFRED D SNOW

In my teenage years I often called in to visit one of the older men of the village, 'Big Patsy' Doherty. During the winter months, Patsy was generally laid up, and it wouldn't be uncommon to have to call down to his bedroom, where he was stretched out resting a painful hernia. His wife, the 'Madonna' as he always called her, or his daughters Agnes or Anne Maria, would usher me in and then leave us in peace. He would ask the local news but within minutes he would fall to reminiscing, about the fishing, about his time on the 'Mudboat' (the Waterford harbour commissioners' dredger called the *Portlairge*) or some seafaring tale or other. One that stands out was the story he told that started out with the curious question, 'Did ye know that the expression "dauntless by name, dauntless by nature" has a particular meaning with the men of the harbour?'

The story started on a storm-tossed morning on 4 January 1888 when an American sailing ship was driven into Waterford harbour. She was the *Alfred D Snow*, a three-masted fully rigged timber sailing ship, built in the Samuel Watts shipyard in Maine, USA. Sometimes her type was referred to as a 'Down Easter'. She was 232ft long with a beam of 42ft. Having loaded bags of wheat and flour at the port of San Francisco in August, she sailed out the golden gate and turned south through the roaring forties, around the Horn and then sailed east, surging through the South Atlantic's enormous 'greybeards', towards Europe.

Her skipper was Captain William J. Willey, on his last trip in the ship, which he had agreed to take to pay for a new home. Among the other twenty-eight souls aboard were Willey's 18-year-old nephew, John, and a crew of mostly Americans, but also men from England, Ireland, France, Germany, Norway and Russia.

She seems to have had fair weather on the trip but according to the ship's log, which was later found on Wiley's body, she had been taking water for some time. As she came towards the Irish coast, a south-east gale started to blow. The crew battled bravely but in vain and as the storm grew in force they were swept towards the last place a sailing ship wants, a leeward shore. In desperation they were forced to seek shelter in Waterford Harbour. She rounded the Hook on the morning of 4 January 1888 and was seen from Dunmore East at about 9 a.m.. Her sails were dropped, leaving her without much helm, and they tried to inch the ship in under the Hook Peninsula in an effort to find shelter.

On land people were waking up from a terrible night of wind and sleet showers. The wind was reported to have gone south-south-west but it was still a gale. As the ship inched further up the harbour and closer to the Wexford shore, those watching were helpless to give direct assistance. The tide had now turned ebb, meaning that it flowed against the ship and against the seas driven in by the Atlantic. She was also reported to be deep in the water, meaning that she was unlikely to sail over the sand bar above Creaden Head as the tide dropped. Although the ship had been spotted in Dunmore East, the lifeboat would not respond until much later. The local paddle tug *Dauntless*, which operated on behalf of the Waterford Steamship Company, did try to respond. A telegram reached Passage East and Captain Cotter immediately departed.

The *Dauntless* bravely battled the mountainous seas and she was like a cork on the crest of the waves before disappearing in a mad downward drive into the trough. The men aboard were all local and, although they knew their own craft was in serious jeopardy, they would not give in. Most of them had lost someone to the sea and knew how critical it was to try to reach the stricken vessel.

Here Patsy paused as the tea was brought in, and he had to taste it and reassure his waitress that it was to his liking. I was given tea and biscuits, and warned not to give any to the big man as they were bad for him. I couldn't wait for the girls to leave and the story to resume. Patsy, for his own reasons, was keen to see them gone too; he loved a biscuit, but only if there was no cake.

Before the *Dauntless* could get close to the *Alfred D Snow*, a massive wave struck her and damaged one of her paddle wheels. Manoeuvrability was hampered and it was all Captain Cotter could do to keep his little craft bows on into the seas as she was driven back up the harbour.

The crew of the *Dauntless* could clearly see the sailing ship was now grounded, and much too far from the shore for any land-based rescue. From a distance they witnessed the ship heeling on to her side, the waves crashing aboard, and the desperate efforts of the crew to launch a ship's boat. This they lowered into the sea with some difficulty and boarded it. It remained sheltered by the hulk of the stranded vessel, tethered by rope. But eventually, in desperation of their situation, the rope was released and they put their fate in reaching shore. The onlookers on the *Dauntless* were helpless, however, as it was swamped and all aboard were drowned.

During the days that followed, pieces of the wreckage floated in all along the harbour; these were secured by the coastguard and later auctioned off to recoup the owner's loss. Timbers were used in the making of the Strand Tavern in Duncannon, and the bar of the Ocean Hotel in Dunmore. They were also used in house construction throughout the harbour and I believe a table from the ship was taken from the tide by a Cheekpoint fishing family and for many years after had pride of place in the living room. One of the more interesting artefacts that was salvaged was the ship's figurehead. It was for many years the property of Captain Richard Farrell, former harbour master of Waterford, and it stood in his front garden. I understand it was sold during the 1980s to a London antiques dealer.

Of the crew, several bodies were washed ashore but identification was difficult. Captain Thomas of a sister ship of the company travelled over from England and I understand identified three of the men: Captain Willey by a ring on his finger, ship's carpenter John Learmond, from the measuring stick that was found in his pocket, and the mate, Patrick Sullivan. I believe all three were returned home for burial, transported in lead-lined, brandy-filled caskets. Willey and Learmond were interred in Thomaston Cemetery, Maine.

The remaining bodies were interred in Ballyhack grave-yard, where a memorial plaque was erected at the entrance by students of Ballyhack National School in 2016.

But not everything perished aboard the ship that fateful day – the ship's dog, a red setter named Dash, managed to swim to shore and climbed up the rocks to safety. He lived for many years after in the care of the Ivie family from the Woodstown area. And Captain Willey's wife also survived. Contemporary newspaper articles reported her death while accompanying her husband on the trip (a common enough practice at the time). However, Cordelia Willey remained behind with her family: a son named Walter (who would later become a sea captain too), and two daughters. Cordelia would eventually be buried by her husband's side following her death in 1913.

At an inquiry into the sinking held later that month and into the first few days of February, a very difficult and at times highly charged hearing took place that sought to explain the failure to launch the Dunmore lifeboat and whether the lack of a pilot boat on station was a contributory factor.

The pilot boat had travelled up to Passage on the previous night to seek shelter from the gathering storm. The next morning, as the *Alfred D Snow* came into harbour, she was still in Passage and even if the ship had signalled for a pilot by raising the necessary flag in her rigging (which she didn't), no pilot could have been put aboard.

Captain Christopher Cherry, who was coxswain of the Dunmore East Lifeboat *Henry Dodd* on the morning of the disaster, faced stiff questioning about his failure to go to the rescue. Many witnesses deposed as to his neglect of duty, and to the merits of the craft he had on hand to launch for the rescue. However, Cherry was an old sailor, an ex-pilot and pilot boat master who knew the harbour and the sea. He was adamant that he had to make a call on the morning, and even though he had launched in higher winds, he judged from his years of piloting and fishing that the lifeboat could not have protected her crew from certain death owing to the tidal conditions and seas that were running that morning. The lifeboat eventually put to sea later in the afternoon with a temporary crew.

Although the inquiry censured Cherry for refusing to sail, I never heard a bad word said against him in Cheekpoint growing up, and certainly Big Patsy never mentioned it either. I suppose men who had spent a life at sea or fishing in the rivers preferred not judge another who had to make so difficult a decision on that fateful day.

Maybe in the end it was as well to remember, just as Big Patsy did, those that tried against all the odds to reach the stricken vessel, and that's probably why I still vividly recall the day I first heard of the brave crew of the *Dauntless*; dauntless by name, dauntless by nature!

Although I recall much of this story from Patsy's original telling I have read and written much in relation to it since. Particular sources that I have drawn heavily on include:

Information on the Willey family from private correspondence with Betsy White, great great granddaughter of Captain Willey.

Much of the specific details of the ship are taken from John Power's book, *A Maritime History of County Wexford*

Vol. 1. 1859–1910 (2011) Olinda Publications, Kilmore Quay, pp. 286–288.

Information was gleaned from contemporary newspaper reportage and specifically on the subsequent inquiry from the *Waterford Standard*, Saturday, 4 February 1888, p. 3.

8

QUARANTINE STATION

There is one particular spot on the river that scared me as a youngster. It is only a square concrete step located on the Waterford side of the shore just above Passage East that looked, and indeed still looks, totally out of place. The slab is surrounded by rock and low-hanging trees, naturally stunted by the tideline. The location is known simply as the Hospital, but it is actually the last remains of an old landing point to the quarantine station; a place where sick sailors could be held under observation. Its function was to try to contain the spread of deadly illnesses into Ireland such as cholera and typhus by holding ships and sailors under observation and isolation before entering the ports of Waterford and New Ross.

My first introduction to it was as a youngster driftnet fishing for salmon, where the concrete feature was used as a marker. Little specific detail was given about the place, but a consistent message we received was to never set foot ashore. We were warned that the diseases it protected the towns from could still be contracted from snooping around the place. Bubonic plague was often referred to, a highly infectious condition that was reputed to have led to the abandonment of a village in Faithlegg. Those who caught it were said to turn black and bleed to death. It was a story that had the power to instil fear.

There was a time when any ships calling to the harbour had to be held at Passage and Ballyhack until they were cleared by customs to continue upriver to Waterford and New Ross. Captains were required to report the health of the ship's company, and any sick sailors were expected to be declared, either to the custom officials directly or by the hoisting of a flag (the yellow jack), which led to an inspection. At times a punt was rowed out to the vessel and the sailor, or sailors, were taken ashore to the hospital. On other occasions the crew were left aboard their vessel and the ship herself was quarantined allowing no connection with land or other ships. I had heard that the anchorage at Buttermilk Castle was specifically used for such cases.

Quarantine as a medical intervention has a long history, most probably originating with steps to counteract the Black Death in Europe in the fourteenth century, a plague that led to the loss of millions of lives. The concerns for shipborne diseases grew, and from the early 1700s laws were enacted in the UK and Ireland to protect ports and citizenry. In some cases ships were used to guard harbours, being anchored in strategic spots. Evidence about the hospital at Passage East, however, is scarce, and apart from the local folklore (always in my experience containing many grains of truth), little seems to be written about the building or its history.

The earliest official mention I can find of the need for a quarantine station at Passage East was a government document of 1824.[28] A quarantine station is listed as being in operation at Passage East in 1828, along with facilities at all major ports including: Poolbeg in the harbour of Dublin, Warren Point in the harbour of Newry, near Garmoyle in the harbour of Belfast, Tarbert in the River Shannon, Baltimore and White Gate in Cork, Green Castle, Lough Foyle and Black Rock, Galway Bay.[29]

In 1832 there is a reference to a ship called the *Lord Wellington* under Captain Culleton of New Ross calling to Passage East. While there, three of his passengers died aboard ship of cholera. He was ordered to sail for Milford Haven to perform quarantine, where it was said three more had died on the trip and another two perished on the quarantine ground.[30]

Another report of the same incident[31] states that, having arrived at Passage, as many as 100 passengers fled the ship in fear for their lives. Three of those who landed at Passage subsequently became unwell and, following the intervention of a clergyman, a temporary hospital was established. A fourth person was discovered lying in a ditch outside the village, and he died not long afterwards. The majority of the passengers, who got away, returned to their homes. Whether they survived, however, is not known, but cholera swept the nation in 1832 and there were widespread deaths. The report certainly confirms that at that stage no official hospital was in place.[32]

The earliest mention I could find of a tangible building in the newspapers is 1866, when something described as a 'Cholera Shed' was located in Passage East. In 1884[33] the hospital was under the control of the Waterford Board of Guardians, perhaps best known for overseeing the operation of the workhouses and administering the poor laws throughout the country on a county by county remit. A newspaper article reports on a meeting of the Board, which was making efforts to take charge of the quarantine hospital. A

Dublin-based firm had either renovated or rebuilt the building at the time at a cost of £205 and it was capable of accommodating sixteen beds.

I found reports in the local papers to be confusing during this period. At times the issue of cholera is a major concern and the hospital is seen as crucial to the health of the country. At other times it appears the building is being leased out to other interests, at one point in 1892 serving as a mortuary, presumably for seafarers.

A news report from June 1905 in the *Waterford Standard* covers another meeting of the Board, and the minutes reveal a letter received from the workhouse, seeking permission for sick children to be allowed to attend what is called Passage Hospital. The Board, we learn, is no longer in charge. The hospital had passed to the control of the Waterford and New Ross Port Sanitary Authority in 1904.[34] In 1910 there was a dispute amongst members of this body; the building is referred to as an intercepting hospital at this point.[35] Following a cholera outbreak in Russia and three cholera-related incidents (on two separate ships in London, for which a quarantine hospital was located close to Gravesend, and an incident in Italy), a circular was issued from the Local Government Board of Ireland urging the need for up-to-date disinfecting devices to treat the clothing and bedding of quarantined sailors. A heated debate is reported, but no decisions are forthcoming. It probably didn't inspire confidence in the newspaper's contemporary readers to learn that a subcommittee was to be formed if and when any cases arose.

The most recent mention in a newspaper comes from 1949.[36] Then the hospital, which was under the control of the

Waterford and New Ross Port Sanitary Authority, has passed to the control of the health authority. I can only imagine that it was allowed to fall into disrepair from that point on. Now little remains but a few bricks on the ground, and of course the concrete step on the river.

Interestingly enough, the local lore states that the building was converted for use during the Emergency (elsewhere known as the Second World War) as a field hospital. The hipped roof had two red crosses painted on either side. No one seemed to know if it had seen any use, and contemporary newspapers I have looked at are silent on the period.

Eamon Duffin, local poet, writer, musician and craftsman, shared a story with me some time ago that fits very well with the accounts of my youth. It was a recollection of a fishing trip in the 1950s with his grandfather of the Rookery, Cheekpoint:

> I remember calling in there with my grandfather, Jimmy Duffin, on the way back from salmon fishing. There was a concrete landing stage with iron railings. The building was of rusting galvanised sheets. You could see old iron beds with bedclothes and pillows thrown on them and on the floor. There were bottles and jars and dressings strewn about also. That was as far as we got as my grandfather said that, 'you wouldn't know what you'd catch if you went in.' …

The power of these stories ran deep in me, too. The site of the hospital is now on private grounds. But I understand from a man living nearby that the remaining structure was taken down and reused in the last few decades. Apparently the site is now practically invisible, apart from a few broken bricks strewn on the ground. The metal railing that Eamon mentioned is long perished too, and steps along with it. It is now little more than a memory, a place name and a concrete slab by the river. An important concrete slab for what it signifies nonetheless, I think.

9

SAILS AHOY HOBBLERS

(IN MEMORY OF LENNY NEILL, 1968–2009)

I would imagine not many would now know what or who the hobblers were. Their lives were once as important to a harbour area such as Waterford as the ships that provided the trade. The hobblers, you see, were the boatmen who supported shipping, and in different eras looked after port essentials such as pilotage, mooring and stevedoring.

On the etymology, a relative in England, Carmel Golding, told me that her nineteenth-century dictionary says it's derived from the Dutch *hobbelen*; to toss or rock about. Further on, hobbler is defined as an unlicensed pilot, also a hoveller, a casual dock labourer. On the south coast of England 'hoveller'[37] was a description of the craft or men that sailed as far as Land's End in search of incoming ships in need of a pilot to safely guide them to port.

In an Irish context, the term hobbler was also widely used in and around Dublin,[38] Belfast and some other east coast ports. I'm guessing that the word was brought by sailors to our shores, although when I have introduced the term before, the more pragmatically minded draw parallels with horses being hobbled to stop them wandering off, and prisoners who needed to be moved had their ankles 'hobbled' so that they could shuffle along but not run away. It's not a huge leap to see a connection to men who came alongside ships and offered to secure them in port.

According to my father, the local understanding of a hobbler was an individual member of a team of men who rowed down the harbour in punts and vied with each other to have the right to guide a ship into Waterford or New Ross. He admired them as hard-working, tough and resilient men who could row miles off the Hook to engage a craft. In the age of sail they could tow a ship past Cheekpoint up through the King's Channel and into the city. They also took the ships via the River Barrow to New Ross. Crews were made up from all the villages and the towns and the competition between crews was fierce.

The method of securing the right to take charge of a ship has variations in its telling. Some said that it was a straightforward race; the first hobbler team to get a rope aboard the incoming vessel secured the prize. However, I have also heard that bidding wars took place with unscrupulous ship's masters, when conditions allowed. Competing hobbler teams would bid and counterbid, undercutting each other, which resulted in bad feeling, scuffles or much worse. My father had one story of a man named Whistler who over time had lost almost all his teeth in various rows with other hobblers. As my father had it, you would hear the Whistler coming because of the wind blowing through the gaps in his damaged teeth!

Other sources have claimed that sometimes the hobbler's function was to be first to an incoming vessel, which won the crew the right to tie the ship up once she got into port. Others talk of winning the right to discharge or load ships.

Another function was, like a modern-era tug boat, to move ships from moorings to berths and vice versa.

It would seem that the hobblers were also employed to get sailing ships through the local bridges. The term for such a procedure locally was 'warping'. A sailing ship on approaching impediments such as the Barrow railway bridge or the tolled Timbertoes Bridge in Waterford city would heave to. The crew would then pass a rope to the hobblers, who would run it through two buoys that were anchored in place above or below the bridges, depending on which way the ship was journeying. Each buoy had an eye atop. The rope was passed through these eyes by the hobbler crew and retaken aboard, effectively doubling the rope. As the ship drifted through the bridge the rope was used to steer and control her passage by the crew.

Another curious aspect of the hobbler story is that in Cheekpoint one theory of the site known locally as 'the Lookout' was also linked to them and employed as a crude but effective signalling system within the port. It's an unproven account, but with local stories, map markings or actual buildings of lookouts at locations as varied as Dunmore, Hobblers Rock at Creaden, Spy Hill in Crook and Popes Towers in Waterford, it is a tantalising theory nonetheless.

Another tangible link to these men is a place name located on Creaden Head, close to Dunmore East and known as the Hobblers Rock. The feature is on the upper side of the headland, in a sheltered spot, and was a departure point for the hobblers and their boats. Tommy Sullivan, an older native of my home village, recalled to me recently seeing two hobblers from New Ross in a small punt operating from there as late as the 1950s.

With the formation of the Waterford Harbour Board in 1816[39], piloting became more organised and pilot boats were employed to put recognised pilots aboard ships. This must certainly have impacted the role of the hobbler, but not completely. (I've seen accounts of hobblers piloting as late as 1894 and there was many a ship's master who probably objected to paying for pilotage and would seek a better rate from the hobblers.)

In my own opinion, the reason that so many definitions or accounts of hobblers exist is because the stories I have heard come from at least two hundred years of maritime trade. Their roles altered as times changed, perhaps initially with the formation of the Harbour Board and the formalisation of pilotage. Increases in sailing ships with auxiliary engines and steam boats must have been the next phase.

Perhaps the most enduring link with the hobblers we had in Waterford up to this year was a family name. The family were the Neills of Waterford, Lenny Snr and Jnr. But both have passed on within months of each other. Lenny Snr had been sick for some time, but his son was operating as a boatman and tug operator in the harbour up to the last. He drowned last spring in a tragic accident and with him perhaps the last that could truly say they were a hobbler in the town. For Lenny was the last as far as I am aware of the Hobbler Neills.

Perhaps in time even the name Hobblers Rock in Creaden will disappear from use, but to me it is a very important maritime place name connection with the port of Waterford and New Ross' past. A point from which I'm sure men had a lookout post, and from where a wary eye was kept on the horizon, and hardened boatmen waited impatiently for a sail to be sighted and the excited cry to go up of 'sails ahoy hobblers'.

10

EVER WATCHFUL COAST GUARD

Below Cheekpoint village a stony strand sweeps out along the river towards Passage East and the deepening harbour. It can be walked when tidal conditions allow for at least a mile, at which point you must retrace your steps or climb the Coolbunnia hillside. As an adult it seems to me we spent each and every Sunday morning of our childhood walking along it, but of course it was only when the tides allowed and the weather co-operated.

My father invariably was nursing a hangover, and following a breakfast of tripe boiled in milk and onion, my mother would whoosh us out of the house, and a-walking we would go. My father was usually joined on these walks by Paddy 'Batty' Doherty and, just like the inevitability of the tides, the stories would flow.

Along the shoreline we would come to a ramshackle old house and quay, which went by the name of Ryan's. It was then lived in by a woman named St Ledger, who had a daughter named Geraldine Turner and a granddaughter named Mary. The house was surrounded by trees and hedges, and only the top of the two-storey house and roof could be seen, and the gable of a boat house. Paddy would often set to reminiscing about an earlier owner and a time when the house and quay were maintained and vibrant. The name Ryan was, of course, a few generations old at that point. Originally they were fishing folk, who operated a weir on the Wexford side of the river, but my interest was piqued when customs men and smuggling were mentioned because one of the family was part of the coastguard, based there to maintain a watch on the ships that plied the rivers to Waterford and New Ross.

Now smuggling is probably as old as the stones on the strand, but the coastguard service was created in 1822[40] in an effort to contain illegal trade. It saw an amalgamation of a number of services and roles including revenue cruisers (boatmen), riding officers (men on horseback who rode the coastline) and the preventative waterguard (shore-based officials who managed incoming and outgoing ships). Their job was simple to define, but hard to execute: to tackle incidents of smuggling and to enforce the collection of taxes.

At the time Waterford was in the top three ports of the country and required a significant force to patrol the coast and the harbour entrance. The administrative base for the ports of Waterford and New Ross was the city, but the operations were at their busiest at Passage East and Ballyhack.

The problem with countering smuggling at the time was that it was seen as a legitimate way to do business. Local merchants saw it as a valid and just way of engaging in trade when seen against the harsh taxes and controls placed on Irish merchants by the English authorities. The smugglers used a variety of methods: hiding contraband in legitimate cargo, running shiploads of illicit cargo, transferring cargo to others such as fishing boats or calling to out-of-the-way drop-off points along the coast and harbour to offload part of their cargo. The enforcement of tax collection and the prevention of smuggling then required a vast force.

A government paper of the 1820s[41] gives a list of the roles employed in the harbour, the numbers employed (ninety-two men), and the costs associated with maintaining the coastguard service at Waterford and New Ross. The top was shared by two positions, the collector and the comptroller, whose chief duty seems to have more to do with keeping each other in check than overseeing the collection of tax (a seemingly regular enough practice within the structure of the organisation). Under them were several clerks, storekeepers and surveyors to ensure the smooth administration of a vast network of river-related roles. The office of Waterford was housed in the customs house, a building that was based on the quays close to the present clock tower. There was a sub-office in New Ross with another customs house and smaller depots or positions at Arthurstown, Dunmore and, of course, Cheekpoint. The principal base of operations was at Passage East.

Passage was an obvious choice, due to its strategic location. Ships could reach the village under sail without too much difficulty, and anchor there to await unloading by the lighters (flat-bottomed vessels), sailing when tide and wind allowed, or towing to ports by the hobblers, and later by paddle steamers or tugs. First aboard was the tide surveyor (earlier spelled tyde) to check the manifest and cargo and ensure all was in order. The particulars of the ship's cargo and journey were taken for record. A tide waiter (wayter) was left aboard the ship to ensure that nothing was removed from the vessel, and he would stay with it day and night. The waiters would leave if the cargo was moved to a lighter, or remain aboard and travel upriver if the ship headed to Waterford or Ross. Once arriving in port, the waiter presented himself to the custom house to account for the cargo, the unloading being carried out by porters, supervised by landing waiters, and these under the supervision of land surveyors.

A fleet of boatmen and craft serviced the coastguard, ensuring ease of transport to and from vessels and between the lower harbour and the ports. Meanwhile, along the coastline further watchers were stationed. These included coast officers and walking officers, and also riding officers. Between them they would keep a watch on approaching ships and would effectively follow them along the coast to Passage or Ballyhack, handing over responsibility and providing any observations to the surveyor on duty. The most numerous employees were working as tide waiters and supernumerary (standby position) tide waiters, which numbered forty-two men alone.

Try as the coastguard might, the numbers of vessels and the ingenuity of sailors and merchants created a constant supply of smuggled goods. It would take a fundamental shift in government policy towards free trade and fairer taxes later in the nineteenth century before the problem started to be effectively addressed, although not ended.

It would be easy to imagine the need to supervise the anchored ships off the shore and the constant checking and rechecking as boats came alongside. Ryan's house and quay would have offered a bird's eye view. Paddy, of course, had lots of tales of lads that had got away with smuggling through a wide variety of means. Nets were brought in from the UK by returning sailors; and parts for bikes and contraband

during the war years if it could be got, such as fruit or tea—
stuff that was either rationed or impossible to get. Some was
dropped off the stern of ships such as the *Great Western* or the
Rockabill as they travelled back to Waterford from Fishguard
or Liverpool, before the customs men could intercept the
sailors coming ashore. They always said the first outboard in
the village came home in the sleeping bunk of a local sailor.

All the yarns were just grist to the mill with me, and I have
to admit I was always drawn to the cool crafty characters
who by dint of sheer intelligence managed to outsmart the
authorities. My father had a great one about a chap who
worked as a dockworker on the Liverpool quays. The customs men and harbour officials were always after him, sure
in the knowledge he was smuggling but never able to find
anything on him. Try as they might, they would stop him and
search him, asking him to turn out his pockets but always
to no avail. My father chanced seeing him one evening in a
pub when on a spree ashore. The dockworker was sitting at
the bar and was approached by another chap. They chatted,
money was put into the hands of the dockworker under the
bar, who then got up off the seat and left, leaving his overcoat
behind on the back of his stool. The chap took the dockworker's seat and, having finished his drink, he got up and
left – but not before taking the overcoat and putting it over
his shoulder. The customs men in the morning were different
from the lads in the evening, and so never realised he never
wore an overcoat to work, only going home!

11

LONG-LEGGED
SPIDER LIGHT

There is one particular feature that stands apart in the harbour area that always intrigued me. It's a seven-legged lighthouse known as the Spit Light or the Spider Light, and it marks a sandbank known as the Spit that reaches out from the Passage East side of the harbour and provided a signal to allow safe navigation through the channel outside of it.

Now as a child I probably only saw the Spider Light a handful of times from shore. These were fleeting glimpses, but enough to capture my imagination. I always considered it to be a magical structure, its shape reminding me of a gigantic house spider that had fled its home and ran along the strand, only to freeze as it put its long spindly legs into the waters of the harbour. Maybe I fantasied about it more because nothing was ever made of it. When we drifted downriver it was rarely if ever as far as the Spit and so it was out of sight and reach, and also probably taken for granted by the fishermen.

Its position meant more to me the first year I went to drift for herring down the harbour in the local half-decker motor fishing boats. Cheekpoint boats always rounded the light on their journey out of the harbour, whatever the time of tide.

The Passage East boats generally went inside it when tides were favourable, with their local knowledge of a channel that others didn't seem to possess. The light signalled to me the first point where you could feel the rivers changing and the reality of the deeper waters that lay ahead. I was always drawn to its scale and red-painted housing, and the sight of gulls and cormorants perched atop its handrail. As it blinked out its warning light, we passed away down and on wild evenings I firmly believed that I wouldn't be truly safe until I had passed it back on our return journey later that night.

According to the Lighthouse Directory, the Spider Light was operational from 1867, one of four built in the country using an innovative technique that allowed construction on such flimsy surfaces as the mud and sand of the spit. It was lighted before, however; an earlier map of 1787 shows a light perch was in place on the same spot for the guidance of ships.[42] A ship inbound at Duncannon could use it as its next navigation point, ensuring it stayed well clear of the West Banks and its shallow waters.

In 1866[43] the harbour commissioners got permission to construct a new light from the London-based Board of Trade, which governed all maritime matters. The commissioners were allowed to charge an extra ¼d per ton for every vessel coming up to Duncannon and above to pay for its maintenance. A number of plans had been submitted for the construction, one costing £2,500, another £2,000. The former bid was approved as it was considered to 'be the speediest got up, and the best'.

The man whose design it is based on, and who won a worldwide patent for the building technology used, was a Dublin-born engineer named Alexander Mitchell.[44] His patent was known as the 'Mitchell Screw Pile Mooring System', or in modern parlance the 'Helical Pile', and has been since used worldwide in the building of lighthouses, bridges and piers, etc. It was specifically for use in locations with soft surfaces such as sand and mud, where strong tidal conditions meant that a solid foundation for traditional building techniques was impossible. His technology was said to be inspired by the use of a corkscrew.

Although the building technique itself is basic, it took a number of months to complete. First a working platform was positioned on the chosen site. Each pile was then individually screwed vertically into place by a team of men working a capstan winch. As they worked, they sang sea shanties, helping no doubt to keep the rhythm going and to take their mind off the back-breaking grind of the task. Mitchell, although completely blind since the age of 22, was generally in the thick of the work. Once the piles were driven on the corners of the site, a central pile was driven to complete it and then other elements were added to raise the platform well clear of the tides, and upon this the light platform was constructed.

I always thought that Mitchell might have worked on the lighthouse, but recent correspondence with Charley McCarthy of Dundalk suggests that the builder was a man named George Wells of Westminster. He may have been subcontracted by Mitchell, who was unwell at this stage; I'm just not sure. The contract was awarded in April 1866 and Wells was given six months to deliver the project.

In January 1867 two positions were filled for a lighthouse keeper and assistant on the Spit. Following interviews the pilot committee appointed Michael Power of Kyser Street in the city to the main post on a salary of £50 per annum. A vote was needed to decide on his assistant. John Barry lost out to Edward Connors, who received an annual salary of £25.[45]

Originally the light was set to always show red to incoming ships alone, however a green lens was later added to illuminate the channel for ships sailing downriver, marking the position between Seedes Bank (Wexford) and the western (Waterford) shore.[46]

In 1895,[47] the commissioners were of the opinion that following the death of the principal light keeper, Michael Power, one man was sufficient to keep the light maintained. Whether this cost-saving measure was agreed or not, I'm not sure. However, a report from 1914 suggests that the light was automated at that point.[48] An Aga lighting system was decided on as it would provide a much brighter light. It was a new system that saved on fuel (acetylene gas) by having an intermittent light and a sun valve that shut down the light in daylight. It also required less maintenance and didn't need a full-time keeper on hand.

When I spoke with Eddie Fardy recently, he recalled that during his time as part of the buoy gang in the Harbour Board he had worked to upgrade the working platform of the light in the 1960s, from timber to concrete, but in recent years the light has fallen into disrepair. A replacement light pole now marks the Spit, and I fear that this unique and historic structure will not be with us for much longer. That would be a great pity.

12

CAPTAIN BURNS AND THE SCHOONER *BI*

As a native of Cheekpoint, I've often met people both at home and abroad with positive memories about the village or its inhabitants. It's usually a connection with an individual but also recollections of views from the Minaun, the meeting of the three sister rivers, or a meal in the local pub/restaurant, the Suir Inn. So on first meeting a lady in Kilkenny some years back at a picnic lunch, I was taken aback when on hearing my home place, she remarked, 'Oh the people who pillaged the Schooner *BI*!'

Anyone growing up in the village knew the story of the Schooner *BI*. The ship was then a wreck on the Strand Road, her broken ribs and keel covered in seaweed and river mud. She was lying parallel to the road, directly opposite a garage owned by Jim 'Dips' Doherty. We would also know her story, retold often through a poem, written by Bill O'Dwyer. I recall no better recitation of it than by Matt 'Mucha' Doherty, which would have easily graced any stage in the world. It went as follows:

CAPTAIN BURNS AND THE SCHOONER *BI*

I'll sing you of a gallant ship that sailed o'er the western seas,
Whose flag has braved for seventy years the battle and the
    breeze.
She was built in 1867 when Parnell was just a boy,
She was christened at first the Sarah Anne, but later renamed
    the *BI*.

She tramped the Atlantic far and wide, and sailed the Pacific
    too.
She has seen many weathers and many a gale and many a
    cargo and crew.
But though long the day the night must come and ships and
    mortals must die.
But the storm at Christmas sealed the doom of that gallant
    schooner *BI*.

She sailed from Arklow, this gallant ship, bound down for the
    English shore.
But she sprang a leak outside Rosslare, and was stranded just
    near Dunmore.
She was towed from Passage to Cheekpoint quay, now her
    hold is no longer dry.
Battered fore and aft that stately craft, that was once the
    schooner *BI*.

With an ugly list on her starboard bow, with her mainsail
    gone and her boom.
Now her guardian angel is Captain Burns, with Darkie as
    non-de-plume.

She was auctioned as scrap and a Tramore man, her trappings
and all did buy.
He promised the Darkie ten shillings a week to watch over
the schooner *BI*.

While the Captain slept one cloudy night, some fellows came
in a boat,
Went aboard the schooner and stole some rope they needed
to fetter a goat.
When the Captain found the loss next day he raised a terrible
cry.
He was scared of what the owner would say of the theft from
the schooner *BI*.

When the owner came and heard the news a wrathful man
was he.
He told the Darkie he was no use, he knew nothing of ships
or the sea.
He cursed like hell and said 'well, my information I'll buy
Five pounds I'll give to arrest the thief that raided the
schooner *BI*'.

Now Captain Burns was an honest man and he resented the
owner's remarks.
He said, 'Since I took charge of your hulk I'm working from
dawn to dark.
I've welts on me feet from walking the deck so pay me my
wages my boy.
And I'll bid you farewell you may go to hell, yourself and the
schooner *BI*.'

Needless to say, the poem has a Cheekpoint bias and my father, when asked, would shrug and say they were hard times. When pushed to explain he would regale us with stories of 'Captain' Burns, who seems to have been a real 'character' and perhaps not the first choice for a watchman.

My Aunt Ellen often joked about the captain's cuteness as he lived directly opposite her in the village. One story she told was of his staggering home of a Saturday night from the pub, but having the presence of mind to open the curtains from the windows. On the Sunday, as people departed to Faithlegg church for mass, Burns was sound asleep in his bed. But later that day when he surfaced for a cure, he would lambast anyone who claimed that he hadn't been to church, 'Shur wasn't I up and gone to Mass before cockcrow, didn't ye see the curtains drawn?'

But back to the story of the *BI*. Boats such as the *BI* had a proud, workmanlike tradition and went where they were required, and they carried what cargos were available. Schooners originated in America, carried two masts and were manoeuvrable and speedy. In fact, I've read that the name originated from the word skim, such as to skim the waves. They were ideally suited to sailing in coastal waters where winds changed constantly and shallow rivers were common, and a ship needed to change tack regularly. By the start of the nineteenth century schooners had spread to Europe and became a favourite for coastal trading.

There are only a few mentions of her in the Irish papers of the era, and she seems to have worked out of Youghal for many years. In September 1925 the *BI* was up for sale in a notice in the *Irish Independent*, her captain was retiring, and details of the boat and sale can be had from a D. Donovan of

Youghal.[49] The Ballybofey and district notes welcomed the *BI* with a cargo of coal, which we are told was a welcome site at Ramelton quay (Donegal), serving as a 'reminiscence of the shipping in the past'.[50]

Her last days of sail were retold by her then part-owner, Bob Roberts. Roberts was a seaman, journalist, storyteller and musician. He had bought the schooner with another man who acted as mate on a journey from Ireland to the UK. As they sailed down the Irish Sea they had put in to Wexford, where apparently her makeshift crew 'jumped ship'. As it was Christmas they had no luck in finding replacements, or perhaps the local sailors had some suspicions about the sea-worthiness of their craft. Roberts and the mate decided to sail as they were, and while crossing to Falmouth they ran into a gale and the ship started to take on significant amounts of water.

They worked for forty-eight hours to keep the boat afloat, taking turns between the helm and manning the pumps, and they must have been relieved men to enter the safe harbour of Waterford. With the help of a pair of hobblers they managed to beach the schooner on Passage Strand, but their hopes for a quick repair job and to set sail again were dashed. Having seen the condition of the hull, the ship was reported by a custom official to the Board of Trade. The two owners decided to cut their losses (they were probably fearful that if ordered to do a proper survey and repair, it would break them). They decided to sell her to recover their costs.[51]

Newspaper adverts carried notice of the sale of the 'Topsail Schooner *BI*' only a few weeks later. The event was to be a public auction on Tuesday, 19 January 1937 at 12 noon.[52] Locally it was said she was purchased by a man from Tramore who had some plans to make her seaworthy again. He moved her to Cheekpoint and appointed a watchman, but he ended up selling what he could salvage from her and left the hulk to rot.

As regards the pillaging remark earlier, I suppose I can understand Roberts' feelings. Having invested his savings in a joint venture to return the schooner to England, he must have felt cheated. The crew, weather and eventually the ship herself turned on him. The custom official and the price of a proper refit must have sealed his opinion of a pretty disastrous venture. I'm sure the fate of the next owner may have been known to him, too. In such a light his badmouthing of the area is probably understandable, but at least he went on to further, and more successful, adventures.

Locally, however, the reputation of the watchman, Captain Burns, and the *BI* is well protected. They live on through the folk memory and the telling of the poem to succeeding generations. I wonder when Bill O'Dwyer wrote it, could he have foreseen that the *BI* would still be recited today and his words are there for succeeding generations to enjoy? I sincerely doubt it. I'd love to know if Bob Roberts knew of it, too. Certainly, I made sure my acquaintance that day in Kilkenny did.

I'm indebted to William Doherty and Pat O'Gorman for information used in this account.

13

COOLBUNNIA BANSHEE ATTACK

Hallowe'en was always a special night in my early childhood. Both my father and mother relished the night, observing rituals that ran deeply in their veins. The modern antics of trick or treat were unheard of. Party games at home were the norm and a tradition of eating barmbrack for tea was observed. Fruit and nuts were freely available and a trip to the bonfire was essential. But ghost stories were also a tradition, the more frightening the better.

My father had a number of jobs to do on the night. One was the making of the snap apple apparatus, basically two pieces of timber with pointed ends crossed. From the centre a string was tied that was then hung from the door frame. On each of the four ends an apple was impaled, and we, with hands behind our backs, had to try biting one as they spun around. Then there was a game where coins were placed in a basin of water. We plunged our heads underwater in an attempt to seize a coin. If you managed it, you got to keep the money.

Another ritual was to drink coconut milk and eat the fleshy inside of the hairy brown shell. Perhaps because our father always told us of eating these in the South Sea Islands, we felt obliged to share his enthusiasm. I don't remember any of us managing more than a sip, and even that with a curled up face. Bairín breac, or barmbrack as it's more commonly called today, was for tea and a much more pleasant ritual. My mother always placed a coin and a ring inside. The ring was meant to bring you luck and good fortune (the girls said it meant you would wed within the year!). Personally I preferred the coin. It signified wealth and, whether I believed it or not, at least I was five pence richer than I had been if I managed to get it in my slice of the currant cake.

Once night had firmly set in, we set off for the village bonfire. All the children had wished in the days leading up to the night that it wouldn't rain. The fire in those days was built on waste ground by the teenage boys and girls, and it would have taken weeks of collecting timber and anything else that would burn.

Before leaving the house the masks were put over our faces. These masks were the product of our own making, generally in school as part of our arts and crafts class. They consisted of a cereal box with eyes cut out, and were hand-coloured, with some elasticated band to hold them in place. Your mask was another reason you didn't want rain as it would literally fall to pieces if it got wet. Arriving home later, the hope was that our father was in form for a ghost story, and one I recall to this day went as follows:

There was a family called Walsh who lived above in Coolbunnia. The man of the house was a fisherman and was renowned for mischief. He was returning home from fishing one night with his eldest son. They were climbing up the lane off the strand when they heard the banshee singing. The son took flight up the lane, but his father stayed behind and crept closer to see her. She was sitting on a rock looking out on the river and in the light of a half moon was combing her hair with a beautiful comb. Below the river glistened with the moonlight until a cloud moved across and the scene went very dark. Now Walsh loved a bit of blackguarding and in the darkness he watched as the banshee put down the comb to fix her hair and in that instant he crept up, snatched the comb and ran away home.

The banshee was well known to us. 'Bean Sidhe', or fairy woman, was said to cry at night when someone was about to die, usually unexpectedly. Many times I heard the older people claiming to have heard her keening in the days before a tragedy. I have to admit the hair often rose on the back of my neck when they related some of these accounts, especially if it was heard and weeks later a letter arrived from abroad to break news of a tragedy. They earnestly believed in such happenings. Some said she was a young and beautiful woman with long flowing silver hair, whilst others likened her to a wizened old hag.

My father continued:

Meanwhile, his son had arrived home and was relating what he had seen to his mother, whose face was changing into a mask of dread. Suddenly the door crashed open and there her husband stood laughing and shouting, his eyes wild with the sport. But as he banged the door shut behind him the howls of the enraged banshee could be heard coming up the lane. His son and wife saw a strange eerie light shining under the door and the screaming outside rose to a furious pitch.

Mrs Walsh ran to her husband and shook him, asking was he mad or what, how could he bring the banshee on their home and her children, that the demon would murder them all. Realising his mistake, her husband barred the door and they then ran to the windows, checking the latches, pulling the curtains across. He urged his son to put what timber was in the house on the fire. The banshee was rushing round the house, checking for a way in. The windows were shook, the door banged and rattled; the light was seen coming down the chimney. The fire was stoked till the flames rose higher. But it was an open hearth fireplace and if you looked up the chimney you could see the sky and they knew that sooner or later the fuel would run out.

They went up into the bedroom where the younger children had been woken from their sleep and all huddled together and started to pray. Outside the roars of the banshee were relentless, and many the home was woken in the area that night, and in those homes prayers were also said. If only they could give her the comb back, maybe she would go on her way. Suddenly the son had an idea.

At this our father jumped from the chair, and we jumped too, our eyes wide:

The comb couldn't be thrown out, what if she didn't see it? But if it could be held out through the window, she would be bound to see it. They considered the dilemma; no one would be foolish enough to stick their hand out the window. Finally they formed a plan. The son retrieved the long metal fire tongs from the kitchen, and his father placed the comb between the iron tongs. Carefully the window was opened a crack and the comb pushed out in clear view.

Moments later the eerie light appeared at the window and the screeching reached a crescendo of rage as the banshee spotted her stolen comb. She grabbed it and the tongs but the boy hung on and a fierce struggle ensued, she pulling with all her demonic strength while the boy hung on to the tongs, terrified it would force open the window, and entering she would kill them all.

At this my father's voice rose and he clapped his hands with a bang and leapt into the air, scaring us senseless. After we settled down again he completed the tale:

All at once she relented and, departing, she could be heard screeching her way up towards the hill of the Minaun, her comb firmly in her grasp.

Exhausted, the family slumped down to the floor and slept where they lay. Next day the neighbours called and asked after the noise of the banshee. No one would believe the account, but on the fire tongs being produced, they had to relent. The long metal arms were twisted and mangled in a fearsome way, as if forged by some manic blacksmith. Word spread like wildfire, and for years afterwards people coming to the village called in to view the tongs and hear the story.

The banshee, my father claimed, having been bested by the Walshes, was never heard in Coolbunnia afterwards! Sleep was hard to come by after such a story, but sleep was required. So, following a scrubbing at the sink, we were marched off to bed. The next day was All Souls, a holy day of obligation. Despite, or maybe because, we had spent a night in pagan ritual, missing mass was not an option.

14

INCREDIBLE SALVAGE
OF *UC-44*

As a youngster I loved anything to do with war stories, tales from comics, books or films, but particularly anything with a local connection. In those days the reality of the numbers of Irishmen who fought against Germany and the Axis powers was still only mentioned in hushed terms. Whether it was army, navy or air force, this was a topic best avoided. But I was in no doubt that the local sympathies were with Britain and tales, particularly from the First World War, about minesweepers and a naval presence in the river were common. The activities of U-boat submarines were mentioned regularly, and there were stories of them surfacing and sailors rowing ashore in dinghies for supplies, or trading drink or cigarettes for fish. My eyes would widen on accounts of them laying mines in the lower harbour or skulking around in the river at night. I tried to imagine the fear of the era and, particularly from a fishing perspective, never knowing what was happening beneath the waves.

One story that was legendary in the harbour was the loss of the German mine-laying sub *UC-44*. The German Navy ordered *UC-44*, under the command of Kapitanleutnant

Kurt Tebbenjohanns, to sea on 31 July 1917 with orders to deploy nine of her eighteen mines in Waterford; the remainder were designated for Cork harbour. She arrived off Dunmore East on Saturday 4 August and lay at the bottom of the harbour until the tide started to run ebb, then she rose silently to periscope depth.

It was about midnight on a calm moonlit night. Her skipper satisfied himself as to their position and gave the orders to start deploying her load. The UC class of sub was a relatively new design and although it could deploy mines from the surface, secrecy was paramount. As the night was so clear and they were initially so close to land, Tebbenjohanns gave the command to submerge. The mines were stored in chutes in the forward section of the submarine. Each mine was dropped individually and the position carefully recorded. As the mine dropped out, the sub floated astern on the tide. As it hit the bottom, a soluble plug held the mine in position, allowing plenty of time for the sub to clear. Saltwater reacted to the plug, which eventually dissolved and released the mine, which floated up to a predetermined height on a wire.

Beneath the mine was a hydrostatic valve that was set to a specific depth, and this controlled the position of the mine. Whatever way the tide was running, it maintained the mine beneath the surface, making detection much more difficult. There the mines waited for an unsuspecting ship to pass over and strike the protruding horns, which triggered an explosion.

While this operation was ongoing, Tebbenjohanns remained in the conning tower, checking the boat's position and plotting his course for Queenstown (Cobh) in Cork harbour. Suddenly he heard and felt a loud explosion and his boat lurched downwards and struck the seabed.[53]

Tebbenjohanns found himself on the bottom of Waterford harbour in the conning tower and was speedily joined by two other submariners: chief engine room officer Johann Fahnster and a young apprentice named Richter. Any attempts to raise the submarine were in vain, and with no communication with the rest of the crew and waters rising around them they were faced with only one choice: to try for the surface, which was 90ft above. All three emerged from below almost as one, but eventually they drifted apart. Miraculously, Tebbenjohanns was pulled aboard a local fishing boat later that morning by Dunmore East fishermen. He was cared for in the home of Mrs Chester and was seen to by Mr Austin Farrell. Later that morning he was turned over to the authorities and began his journey to London and life as a PoW.[54]

Meanwhile, the British Admiralty ordered a salvage operation and it was initiated three days later from the RFA *Racer* under Lieutenant Gauld. Lieutenant Davis was the salvage master and the operation was under the direct command of Commander Heaton. To offer protection to the activity, *ML478* (a naval motor launch that had initially found and marked the submarine's location) was deployed with four armed trawlers. Divers (tin openers) were sent down to locate the exact location of the sub, and her bow and stern were marked with buoys. On the surface, the divers reported the wreck lying at 90ft, lying across the tide with a 70 degree list to her port side. Such was the urgency attached to locating the code books and other paperwork aboard, that an initial attempt was made to get a diver into the sub, which failed.[55]

Davis' plan was to attempt lifting *UC-44* off the bottom and floating her towards Dunmore East. The strategy employed was basic, if complicated given that she was 90ft down. Cables were dropped from a surface vessel, brought under the sub with the help of divers and then brought back to the surface. At low tide, the cables were tightened down to the decks of a salvage barge (*LC1*) and when the tide lifted the barge it also raised the submarine by the same distance. Once the sub was sufficiently off the bottom, the salvage vessel was towed by a tug (*Goole No. 7*) towards Dunmore. Once it touched the seabed again, the operation halted and the exercise was repeated.[56]

In all it took twenty lifts and with bad weather factored in it would be late September before they reached outside Dunmore. At that stage another process called parbuckling, which meant rotating the U-boat, was employed between the two barges to straighten the sub upright before bringing her over the surface of the water and into Dunmore pier.[57]

Once on the surface and safely within the harbour of Dunmore, the water was pumped out and operations started on the next phase. Examinations took place and the Admiralty learned much about the design and capabilities of the submarine. They were keenly interested in the rescued mines and the deployment system. However, it was the log books and other papers that arguably proved the most value. As soon as it was possible to board, Commander R.J. Richards, who was at the time serving as First Lieutenant of HMS *Snowdrop* (a sloop based at Queenstown) entered the sub under the orders of Admiral Bayly and retrieved the valuable documents. In a case secured to his wrist, the papers found their way to naval intelligence in London within twenty-four hours.[58]

The log proved incontrovertibly what many had suspected but had been denied by senior naval personnel. It highlighted how easy it was for Tebbenjohanns and other U-boat commanders to avoid detection and slip through the existing protection of minefields and patrols around Britain.[59] Such information, coupled with the rates of shipping losses, highlighted that Britain and her allies were at risk of losing the war unless the U-boat menace was finally dealt with.

The reluctance to deal with U-boats seems to have been based on a mistaken belief that they were ineffective. Macintyre explains the failure to grasp the U-boat menace by asserting, 'submariners … comprised a breed apart'. The men who operated them endured 'contemptuous refusal of senior officers and their contemporaries in surface warships to take them seriously'. This attitude created a 'mental inertia or lack of imagination of the great majority, making for an obstinate conservatism'.[60]

Some believe the retrieval of *UC-44* actually turned the war for the allies. What is probably true at least is that it helped in the continuing shift in attitudes in naval strategy and personnel, and more ships and resources were provided to tackle the issue. It also arguably contributed to the removal of Admiral Jellicoe as commander of the British navy. The Dover barrage including 9,600 mines was completed, but according to Tony Babb it was the code books that gave the Admiralty their most significant advantage with the convoy system that had been introduced only months earlier. For now they could more effectively anticipate U-boat activities and thus reroute convoys away from where the U-boats were likely located, ensuring a lot more ships safely reached their destination.[61]

An enduring mystery of *UC-44* was what mine actually sunk her, and there have been a number of theories. One simple one was that through a navigational error she struck her own mine. This is the least likely as the sub was moving away from the mines as they were deployed. Another theory was that there was a fault with the deployment system. As we have seen, ordinarily a mine dropped to the seabed, and a delayed release mechanism allowed it to float up on a chain that anchored it in place. If the mechanism was faulty, or indeed had been tampered with,[62] it may have released early and floated into the sub.

A more intriguing theory is that it was all part of a cunning plan by the Admiralty. Some have theorised that following the activities of a sister U-boat, *UC-42*, in July 1917, which had deployed mines in the same area of Waterford, the harbour was closed for two weeks while a sham sweep by minesweepers was conducted. This was in case spies were watching, or indeed U-boats. After two weeks the Admiralty sent a coded signal to say Waterford was cleared, and opened the harbour. Both sides had already cracked each other's codes. When *UC-44* was deployed she was actually sailing into the live minefield of *UC-42*, and this is what sank her.[63] It's a great story, and it may even be accurate, but as with everything in war the truth is often twisted and turned to serve a purpose, so we may never really know. Personally, I prefer the faulty deployment system theory.

When the authorities were finished with learning all they could from *UC-44* she was towed out of Dunmore and unceremoniously dumped outside the harbour. She was a navigational hindrance, however, and she was subsequently depth charged and later lifted and towed further out to sea.

One theory had it that she was brought to Duncannon in Co. Wexford and later used in an extension of the break-water. This seems to have been explained by the author Roy Stokes, who wrote that her engine apparently lay in a garage in Duncannon for years afterwards and, rusted and worn, was dumped into a new breakwater.[64]

As to the fate of the crew of *UC-44*, well she had thirty men aboard on the night that she sank. Tebbenjohanns was the only one to survive. He spent the rest of the war as a PoW and went into banking in Germany after it ended. He served in the next world war, I believe, and lived into the 1960s, but I found little information about him. Richter's corpse washed up on the Wexford shore in the following weeks and was buried in Duncannon. It was reinterred after the war in the German Military Cemetery at Glencree, Co. Wicklow. Johann Fahnster's body was not recorded as ever being found, as far as I am aware. Of the remaining twenty-seven, the sad fact is that whatever bodies that were found in the hull of the U-boat when she was finally brought ashore were never interred. It has been speculated that to bury so many in a cemetery on land would draw attention to the fact that the U-boat had been salvaged and thus lose a military or intelligence advantage to the Germans. As a consequence the bodies of the crew were taken away and buried at sea.[65]

The whole incident was commemorated in 2017 by the Barony of Gaultier Historical Society and the crew were at least at that point remembered. The names that were found of the crew online are as follows.[66]

RANK	SURNAME	CHRISTIAN NAME
Matrose	BARTZ	John.
Ltnt.z.S.d.Res.	BENDLER	Wilhelm
O.Masch.Mt.	BIENERT	Fritz
Heizer	BORGWALDT	K:
Btsm.Mt.d.Res.	BÖTTCHER	A.
O.Matrose	BÜRGER	O.
Masch.Anw.	CLASEN	H.
Ob.Matrose	DÜSING	August
Ob.Masch.Mt.	FAHNSTER	Johann
Heizer	FEHRLE	Erwin
F.T.Gast	GIESENHAGEN	K.
T.Heizer	GOLOMBOWSKI	–
U.Maat	HEUER	Otto
Ob.Btsm.Mt.	HORAND	Hans
Matrose	IDSELIS	Michael
Heizer	KERSTEN	Heinrich
Masch.T.Mt.	KLEIN	Karl
F.T.O.Gast	KRÄMER	A.
O.Masch.Mt.	LEHMANN	R.
Masch.Mt.	MÜLLER	Heye D.
Ob.Btsm.Mt.	PABSCH	J.
Masch.Anw.	RICHTER	W.
Matrose	ROTTSCHALK	Walter
Masch.Mt.	RÖSLER	P.
Ob.Heizer	SCHICKENDANZ	W.
Steuermann	SCHULTER	J.
Masch.Mt.	SCHMITZ	F.
Mt.Ing.O.Asp.	SEIFARTH	Helmut
Matrose	ZIELOSKO	Emanuel

As if to underline how incredibly cruel and unfair war is, there remains a poignant anecdote from Tebbenjohanns' journey to prison that I think is worth relating. He boarded the RMS *Leinster* under military escort for the trip across the Irish Sea from Dublin to Holyhead. He was sitting in the saloon with his British naval officer escort, having a drink, when Captain Birch, the ship's captain, approached the party and remonstrated with them. Captain Birch was aware of the damage caused by the U-boats and had lost many a friend, and he warned that he would clap them both in irons if the German was not immediately confined. Tebbenjohanns was led to his cabin, and there he sat out the remainder of the journey, apparently in an unlocked and unguarded cabin, while his escort went back to the saloon. He'd given his word not to try and escape.[67] RMS *Leinster* would sink following a U-boat attack in October 1918 and the good captain would die, along with 500 other souls.

But Waterford wouldn't have to wait until 1918 to witness how cruel and heartless war could be.

15

REMEMBERING THE *FORMBY* & *CONINGBEG*

Within two days in December 1917, Waterford experienced its biggest loss of local seafaring lives with the sinking of Clyde Shipping's SS *Formby* and SS *Coningbeg*.[68] Of the eighty-three souls who perished, sixty-seven were from Waterford, the harbour and hinterland, and the effects were profound. Growing up in Cheekpoint, it was an event that was mentioned cautiously and never discussed in any detail. There were sensibilities to be considered, and even as a child I understood that it was best to be cautious. Some things are best left unasked.

The SS *Formby* was built by Caledon SB. & Eng. Co. Ltd, Dundee, in 1914 and was considered the flagship of the Clyde shipping company. She was 270ft long, of 1,283 tons and had a top speed of 14.5 knots. Although primarily a cattle transport vessel, she could accommodate thirty-nine first-class and forty-five steerage passengers.

The SS *Coningbeg* was originally SS *Clodagh*, built for the Waterford Steamship company by Ailsa shipbuilders in Troon, Scotland, in 1903. When the company was sold to the Clyde shipping Co. in 1912 she was renamed. In 1913 she underwent a total refit. She was also 270ft long, of 1,278 tons and capable of a top speed of 16.5 knots. She could carry between 500–600 head of cattle and eighty-six first-class and seventy-four steerage passengers.

Both ships ran a twice-weekly service to Liverpool carrying passengers, livestock, foodstuff and general cargo from Waterford and returning with passengers and general cargo. The trip took an average of sixteen hours one way and both ships had a reputation for strict timekeeping. As the First World War raged, the ships and crews were constantly in danger from surface or torpedo attacks by German U-boats, or mines while at sea and entering port. Not only did these ships assist the war effort, but they kept both sides of the Irish Sea fed, and more importantly for themselves, no doubt, provided food and an income for their crews' own families.

The ships suffered disruption to their services from U-boats. One example from February 1915 concerned the closure of all shipping on the Irish Sea due to a U-boat threat. The *Coningbeg* was confined to Waterford port, which caused mayhem as her cargo of cattle had to be unshipped and accommodated elsewhere. Meanwhile, the families of the *Formby* gathered on the quay of Waterford under an increasing cloud of fear, as there were unfounded rumours that she was sunk. Later that month, the *Coningbeg, Formby* and SS *Arklow* failed to put to sea due to a dispute between their crews and the shipping company over a war bonus for the risks they were taking.[69]

At 11 a.m. on Saturday, 15 December 1917, the SS *Formby* slipped her moorings and travelled out the Mersey and into the Irish Sea. Aboard were thirty-seven crew and two passengers. What those aboard did not know was that they were being trailed by *U-62* commanded by Captain Ernst Hashagen and that within hours he would blast her out of existence. She was due into Waterford the following morning, but when she did not arrive on time there was only minor concern. Later on Saturday a storm of sleet and snow had developed, becoming a gale overnight, causing widespread damage. In Waterford it was presumed the *Formby* was sheltering and would be into port later on Sunday. She never arrived. As the fears grew it was decided to send a cautionary message to Liverpool to halt the *Coningbeg* sailing. No telegrams could be sent, however, as all the lines were down following the storm.

Having sat out the storm in Liverpool, the *Coningbeg* set sail for Waterford on Monday, 17 December at 1 p.m.. Oblivious to the concerns in Waterford, she departed with a crew of forty and four passengers. Unfortunately, *U-62* had returned to a position off Liverpool and was waiting for them, too. When the ship failed to arrive, pandemonium ensued in the city of Waterford. Immediate family, relatives, neighbours and friends gathered at the Clyde company offices for any scrap of news. Over Christmas the vigil continued but on Thursday, 27 December the company felt obliged to write to each family confirming everyone's worst fears; they could no longer hold any hopes for their loved ones' return.

Of the ships no trace was reported, and no information could be gleaned as to what had occurred. Locally it was considered too much of a coincidence that two fine ships would both disappear within two days of each other, except through hostile action. A special appeal fund was created to provide for the seamen's families until such time as they could qualify for the Board of Trade war loss pension. This was only payable where hostile forces caused the ship to founder, and although this was later accepted as the cause, for some families this was not paid out until 1920. The appeal fund was still in use up to 1927.[70]

SS Coningbeg departs Waterford with a full head of steam up. (Courtesy of the Brendan Grogan Collection)

The dredger *Portlairge*, more commonly referred to as the mud boat. (Courtesy of Jonathan Allen)

Above: The last of the three ships *Great Western* (1933). (Courtesy of the Andy Kelly Collection)

Left: Spider Light (Spit Light), an Annie Brophy photograph. (Courtesy of the John O'Connor Collection)

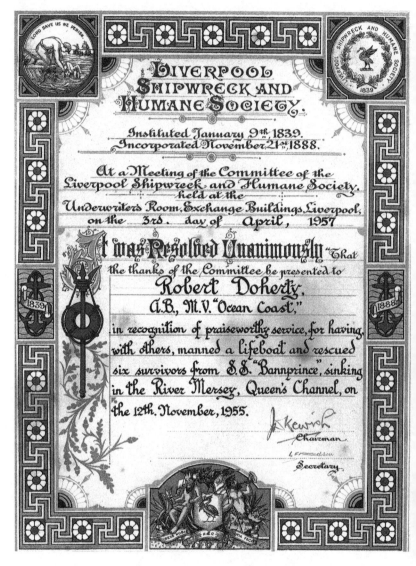

My father's award from the Liverpool Shipwreck and Humane Society.
(Courtesy of Mary Doherty)

In time the body of the *Formby* stewardess Annie O'Callaghan would wash ashore in Wales, apparently the only one to be recovered (or at least positively identified). The remains of two lifeboats and a nameplate of the *Formby* were also recovered. But it would be the publication of Ernst Hashagen's war diary in 1931 that would finally confirm the fate of both ships, blasted from the Irish Sea without any warning, or chance to get to their lifeboats, by U-boat *U-62*. Many, however, were unaware of the diary's existence and the details it contained.

Down the years people still held that the ships were lost in a terrific storm. But on the seventy-fifth anniversary Richard McElwee published his account, *The Last Voyages of the Waterford Steamers*. The book, which goes into significant details about the sinkings and includes excerpts from Hashagen's memoirs, makes for chilling reading. But it also serves to remind the public of the service these sailors gave to the city and the country.

On Waterford's quays today we now have a significant memorial, which lists all the names of those who perished. It was unveiled by the then president of Ireland, Mary Robinson, in February 1997. The crews are also remembered on the Tower Hill Memorial in London to merchant seamen, the Dunmore East memorial wall to Waterford seafarers and fishermen, and the more recent memorial wall in Dungarvan to those who died in the First World War.

Strangely enough, it was McElwee's book that finally lifted the lid on the story at home. I had always guessed my father's reluctance to discuss it was because a neighbour of his from the village, 'Baby' Burns, had lost her father, John, on the *Formby*. 'Baby' was ever present in the village as I grew up and I imagine the reluctance was that no one wanted to draw up a painful subject. It was probably ingrained in my father from his childhood. But with the book came a catharsis, I think. Finally he had something in writing, something tangible about the event. Perhaps even he, finally, had the story straight for the first time in his life.

16

The Night the Devil Came for the Captain's Corpse

Even in a small locality such as Cheekpoint I was often surprised that different people would have so different a version of the same story or event. One that highlights this vividly is a story I was raised on about a visiting ship called the *Honved* dating to the 1930s. My grandmother and mother spoke about it frequently but their account, or rather their emphasis, was on the social aspect of the story. My father, needless to say, had a more entertaining account with a dramatic twist; the story of the night the devil came for the captain's corpse.

The story starts in the summer of 1932, when the MV *Honved* arrived into the port of Waterford with a cargo of Maize for R&H Hall on the North Quays of the city. When the cargo was discharged the ship moved off her berth and dropped down to Cheekpoint, where she anchored while the ship waited for an outgoing cargo. (Following the Stock Market crash of 1930, there was a global shipping slump, and ships struggled to find freight.) To save money, discharged ships awaited a confirmed cargo before setting sail.

The captain of the ship, Rudolph Udvardy, was already ill
when entering port. Nursed by his wife Rosa, who accompanied the ship, he also received medical attention when at
anchor off the Russianside, Cheekpoint. The doctor travelled
over from Dunmore East, and was regularly rowed out from
Moran's poles to the ship by my grandmother's brothers,
who also waited to return him to shore. As a consequence
my grandmother, who was then a young girl (born in 1919),
had a front-row seat of the events.

As the ship had only limited stores, the crew were forced to
forage for food to supplement their diet. In some cases they
signed off the ship and found another vessel. Meanwhile, the
village rallied around the remaining crew. Fish was dropped
alongside, and items such as bread, milk and other supplies
were shared. The crew and Rosa were invited ashore for
dinner or social events.

The event that stood out in my grandmother's account
started one morning as she helped her mother around the
house. As she came out of the house with an ash bucket from
the fire she walked straight into a man. But it was no ordinary
man, or at least like no man she had seen before, for he had
dark skin and long black curly hair. She dropped her ash bucket
in terror and turned to run, but the dark man reached out for
her and started to speak with a strange accent. She managed to
break free just as her mother came out the door. She fled into
the house, into her parents' bedroom and crawled under the
bed. She was still there when her brother Christy came in later
that evening and he finally managed what everyone else had
failed to do, to entice her out from her hiding place.

She told him all about the 'coal man' and how he terrified her, and Christy in turn told her about the Arab sailors

who helped make up the crew of the *Honved* and how their skin was different from our own. Ali, who worked as a stoker in the engine room of the ship, would become a familiar visitor to the house, coming as he did on the instruction of her father to get eggs, vegetables or spuds. She was never comfortable around him, but he used to whistle to announce his coming, which gave her time to get to her mother's side.

On Friday, 2 September 1932, the captain died. The following day, his coffin was brought ashore on a local fishing boat to Cheekpoint quay, and taken by hearse to Faithlegg Church. After the removal ceremony the congregation of mourners dispersed, leaving the captain's coffin at the altar to await the burial.

Later that night the chapel woman, who looked after the church, went to lock the front door. As she was about to close it, she noticed a silhouette near to the altar in the evening gloom. Moving slightly closer, she could hear a low mumbling sound. Terrified, she turned on her heels and ran to her home, the gate lodge to Faithlegg House. There she explained what she had witnessed to her husband and another man, who were sitting at the kitchen table playing cards. There was a lot of talk about the devil coming for the captain; there was a lot of winking among the men, too.

To humour the woman, they agreed to accompany her back to the church. Strolling in, they had a light step, but they froze at the back of the church when they too heard sounds. More cautious now, they scooped up some holy water and began to inch forward, splashing it as they went, hoping the sacred water would be enough to keep any evil away. In the darkness nothing could be seen, but as they inched forward, the mumbling could be discerned as words, strange and foreign words.

Panic was rising among the three and the holy water was being splashed with abandon when one of them stumbled and emitted a cry. All went silent, no mumbling could be heard, and then a whisper came from the area where the captain's coffin stood. Someone was asking who was there, in broken English and in a strange accent, but undoubtedly human.

Moving forward with more certainty, and a significant amount of relief, the would-be protectors of the captain's coffin were confronted by the sight of the Arab crew. They did not hold with the Irish custom of leaving the coffin on its own in the church overnight. Their custom, they explained, was to remain with their dead until burial. Following a brief whispered conference, they decided that the chapel should be left open to allow the crew keep their vigil.

When the captain was finally committed to foreign soil, the grave was surrounded by his remaining officers and crew. And there was a huge turnout from the area, a turnout as befitted a sailor who died so far away from his family. That was an occurrence well known to, and evoking strong sympathies in, a seafaring village such as Cheekpoint.

The ship remained for a few more weeks and finally, with a new captain, the *Honved* sailed out the harbour. Rosa Udvardy had returned home after the funeral and would later send a small tree in a pot, asking that it be planted to mark her husband's grave. It marks it to this day, a strange sight in an Irish graveyard perhaps – a palm tree.

Flowers still appear on the grave from time to time, an indication perhaps of how deep the connection to the events that autumn in 1932 went in a small seafaring community. Or maybe the captain's devoted crew still watch over him to this day?

17

ESCAPING THE 'HELL SHIP'

Sometimes my father's stories made my jaws hang open with shock and surprise. One such time was when looking at a movie on television about the German battleship *Graf Spee*. 'Did you know there was a Cheekpoint man captured by the *Graf Spee*?' he asked. Needless to say I didn't, and instantly that movie faded into the background and my father's voice took centre stage. His account was briefer than mine, but I think it needs all the details I have gleaned since to do it justice.

On 16 February 1940 naval history was made and a major diplomatic incident was triggered when the Royal Navy boarded a ship called the *Altmark* in Norwegian waters. It led to the freedom of 300 merchant sailors, one of whom was a Cheekpoint sailor named Pat Hanlon. It also led to a catch cry that became synonymous with the Royal Navy – 'The Navy's Here', which was taken up by the press and media as a symbol of naval potency.

What became known as the *Altmark* incident began with the pride of the German naval fleet, the *Admiral Graf Spee*. At the commencement of the Second World War she was dispatched to the South Atlantic under the command of

Captain Hans Langsdorff with orders to make war on the allies; merchant and naval ships alike.

Langsdorff belonged to a different era of German Navy sailor, and was probably thought of as old fashioned, because he sought to protect the lives of fellow seamen. As a consequence, the modus operandi of the *Graf Spee* was to approach allied shipping with the French flag at her stern, and once alongside run up her true colours and put a crack boarding party onto the allied ship. The crew were then transferred, or if close to land, were given the option of rowing to shore in their ship's lifeboats. Charges were then set and the ships sent to the bottom. As a consequence, Langsdorff probably sank fewer ships than would have been possible, but of the nine he did sink, no crewman died of which I am aware.

The SS *Newton Beech* of Newcastle upon Tyne (a Tynesider, as my father called it) was built in Sunderland by the Pickersgill & Sons shipyard in 1925. She was an average-sized tramp ship of her day, owned by Tyneside Line, with a crew of twenty-one locals and fourteen from other areas including Cheekpoint. She was under the command of Captain Jack Robinson and had departed Cape Town in late September, heading for her home port with a cargo of maize.

Aboard that fateful morning was Pat Hanlon, one of the eleven children born to fisherman Martin Hanlon and his wife Margaret *née* Murphy, who was originally from Mooncoin in Co. Kilkenny. The family lived in Coolbunnia on the main road into Cheekpoint.

On 5 October, the SS *Newton Beech* was intercepted and stopped, a prize crew boarded her and she was sailed in convoy with *Graf Spee* by that crew. A couple of days later, as the victims of the German raider mounted, the prisoners were transferred off the *Newton Beech* and she was sunk.

As the number of prisoners grew they were transferred to the tanker MV *Altmark*, which shadowed the battleship providing oil supplies. This ship hid under a Norwegian flag and fake name SS *Sogne*. As the allied net closed on the *Graf Spee* and her ultimate fate, it was decided that the *Altmark* would break away from the scene and return to Germany. Working hard to avoid capture, her captain, Heinrich Dau, headed northwards towards the Arctic before turning east towards the Norwegian coast.

Aboard, conditions were tough, but apparently fair. The *Altmark* was a large ship and prisoners were held in various sections, Pat being unlucky to be 25ft down in one of the holds. It was dark, cold and very uncomfortable. At one stage Pat got in trouble as he tried to send an SOS in a tin over the side in the hope of raising the alarm. He need not have worried.

British naval intelligence was aware that prisoners had been taken and was busy trying to track likely vessels. As the *Altmark* approached Norwegian waters, the navy demanded her detention and a proper search. Despite the Norwegian Navy boarding the ship on three separate occasions, nothing was discovered. British suspicions were not allayed, however, and having been tracked down by a spotter plane, the ship was intercepted by the destroyer HMS *Cossack* whilst still in Norwegian waters. The diplomatic tensions were so heated that none other than Winston Churchill himself gave the order to intercept and board the tanker. She ran aground in a fjord and was subsequently boarded by the navy, where hand-to-hand combat was used for fear that stray gunfire would harm the prisoners.

When the hold containing Pat Hanlon was thrown open, he was first up the ladder – and risked falling back off it, such was the surge from below. All the freed prisoners of war were taken aboard HMS *Cossack* and she departed for Leith the following day. The newsreels rolled and the opportunity for propaganda was not missed as footage of the rescue was shown in cinemas all over Britain. (It can still be seen on Pathé news clips on YouTube.)

The incident was widely reported in the media and Pat found himself on the pages of several newspapers, including the *Irish Independent* and the local *Munster Express*. The *Altmark* was described as the Hell Ship, but I'm not sure that is very accurate, or tallies with Pat's account. But then again, it was war, and opportunities for propaganda could not be ignored. It also created history in that it was the last naval boarding undertaken by the Royal Navy. It led to the German invasion of Denmark and Norway two months later, apparently because Hitler determined that the Norwegians were not prepared to stand up to the British on matters of neutrality.

Despite his experiences, Pat returned to sea not long afterwards and he along with hundreds of fellow Waterford men and thousands of Irishmen sailed with the Merchant Navy all through the horrors of the war. Unfortunately, the consideration of Captain Langsdorff was uncommon and tens of thousands of merchant men died. One piece I read put this total at 50,000, some of whom were from Cheekpoint and many more from Waterford and the rest of Ireland. It's worth remembering they put to sea in ships with little or no way of defending themselves and were unsung heroes in a war where they played a crucial part, and got little by way of recognition for their bravery.

Thankfully, Pat survived the ravages of the war and afterwards got married and started a family in Liverpool, where he continued to work as a seaman. He died in Liverpool in 1994 at the age of 89 and his ashes were scattered on the Mersey.

Pat was one of many who served the merchant marine during the war, not all of whom were as fortunate. I suppose because his own father served too, my father had a soft spot for such men and admired them deeply; an admiration he passed on to me.

Much of the story was as given by my father, but other details were accessed from Pat's niece, Anna Phelan, a neighbour of my mother, and also from an article by Con McGrath published in *Ireland's Own* in November 2013 and two specific newspaper accounts based on interviews with Pat: *Irish Independent*, 22 February 1940 and *Munster Express*, 23 February 1940.

18

Barrow Railway Viaduct: A Century of Mishaps and Incidents

One of the most significant architectural feats of engineering in the harbour of Waterford is the Barrow Railway Viaduct. It was built to connect Rosslare with Waterford's Plunkett train station and from there to link into the entire south of Ireland. The designer was Sir Benjamin Barker and the builder, following a competitive tendering process, was the Glaswegian firm of William Arrol & Co. The winning bid was £109,347 and work commenced in early 1902. The project necessitated the tunnelling of Drumdowney Hill and the provision of an opening section that allowed ships access and egress with New Ross port.[71]

In total the bridge is 2,131ft in length and consists of thirteen fixed spans mounted on twin 8ft diameter cast iron cylinders filled with concrete. Eleven spans are 148ft long and the two closest to the opening span are 144ft. The opening had to be in the deepest part of the river channel, thus the Kilkenny side. The bridge was positioned 25ft above high water on the spring tides. Both the bridge and the South West Wexford line were officially opened on 21 July 1906. It was the last major piece of rail infrastructure built in Ireland.[72]

Now as you can imagine, such a bridge and particularly the opening through which sail and steam ship had to pass occasionally caused some dramas. As children we were well acquainted with them. One of my personal favourites as told by my father went as follows:

> Two lads were coming down the River Barrow in a punt, from fishing eels, when they spotted a mine floating towards the Barrow Bridge. As they rowed around the mine, they realised that the tide was taking it towards the opening span wharf and that if it hit it, the whole bridge could explode. Well as they debated it, they heard the noise of an approaching train. Realising that the train was in possible peril, they fashioned a lasso out of some rope. Getting as close as they dared, they managed, after a number of failed attempts, to get the line around the mine. They then rowed away from the bridge, towing the mine behind them. Passengers had rushed to the windows to see why the driver was blowing so frantically on the whistle and on realising what had happened, several passengers fainted, others roared and cheered with relief, while the engine men blew the whistle in thanks the whole way to the Drumdowney tunnel.

The truth was a little less fantastic, but no less dramatic. The men were Jack Heffernan and Jack O'Connor, both of the Rookery, Cheekpoint. The year was 1946 and the Second World War (or Emergency as we called it) had just finished.

As a consequence many dangerous experiences were had with floating mines. What we can discover from the newspapers[73] is that the men spotted the mine floating in the river and when it grounded between Snow Hill Quay and Drumdowney Point (known locally as the Point of the Wood) as the tide went out they rowed across and managed to tie a rope from a tree to the mine, thus preventing it floating away. Courageous in itself.

The daring duo managed to alert the guards at Passage on the Friday afternoon. The newspaper account doesn't say how but I would presume they rowed down to Passage East on the outgoing tide. Either that or they cycled from the village as the public phone box didn't come to Molly Doherty's shop at the crossroads until the 1950s. The authorities alerted, a bomb disposal unit from the Curragh Camp in Co. Kildare was dispatched by truck.

Although the boat train departed from Waterford that evening, it was decided to close off the bridge to rail and shipping on the Saturday and both the morning train to Waterford (6.50 a.m.) and the 9.40 a.m. market train from Waterford stopped and departed from Campile Station in Co. Wexford. Bus transfers were used to get around the situation.[74]

The bomb disposal unit, under Comdt Fynes, had to wait for the tide to go out before they could approach the mine on the Saturday. It was described as 5ft 4in by 3ft 4in and was encrusted with rust and barnacles. It was thought to have been deployed on the seabed with an anchor and chain that had broken away. The opinion of the army was that it had been deployed several years before, but no details or opinions were expressed as to its origin. The unit managed to make safe the mine by 4 p.m. that evening, allowing the 5.30 p.m. boat train to depart Waterford in safety.

Of course, there were many other incidents, the first before the bridge was even operational in 1905. During construction two sailing vessels struck it on the one day, indeed almost at the same time. The ships were the *Conniston* and the *Ethel* under the guidance of pilots Whelan and Kearnes, leaving New Ross on an ebb tide. The Harbour Board received a complaint about the matter from the builders, but thankfully not much damage to the bridge had occurred. The master of the schooner *Ethel* also wrote alleging damage to his ship. The board interviewed the pilot on the matter who explained that at the White Horse reach (just above the bridge on the Kilkenny side close to Ballinlaw) he had recommended to the master that the ship should be warped[75] through the opening. He claimed the master of the *Ethel* refused, stating that the wind was sufficient and he could control the passage through. (The master was probably conscious of getting away on the tide and not wishing any delays.) Approaching the opening, the wind dropped and as he was unable to maintain way on his vessel the master ordered the anchor dropped. This done, the schooner swung to the anchor but she struck the bridge as she did so. No details were given as to the incident with the other vessel.[76]

A few months later, in 1905, pilot Whelan was again in trouble when a steamer under his control struck one of the cylinder piles and dislodged a concrete coping. Despite the evidence of the harbour master (Captain Farady, who was also aboard) that the accident was completely outside the control of his pilot, Whelan received a caution.

The next incident came almost an exact year from the official opening of the bridge:

Yesterday the barque Venus, of Helsingborg, Norway, bound
for New Ross, with a cargo of timber, whilst in the tow
of the barque Heron, collided with the Barrow Bridge, or
Railway Viaduct. The Venus had her whole foremast knocked
clean out, and the crew had a narrow escape, the bridge being
apparently uninjured.[77]

While Dublin was in revolt during Easter 1916, the bridge
was one of the pieces of infrastructure considered vital to the
interests of the crown forces. Admiral Bayly, commander of
the British naval services sea protection detail based at Cobh
(then called Queenstown), sent motor launches to secure the
bridge and ensure uninterrupted rail travel.[78]

In 1923 the opening span was stuck in an opened position
for some days following the loss of a 'shaft' that was central
to the operation of the swivel action for opening the bridge.
The shaft was finally retrieved by dragging the river bed. No
explanation is supplied as to why it happened, or indeed why
a replacement could not be found.[79] My own thought was that
it mirrors a similar incident in Waterford with the Redmond
bridge and other related disruptions on the line in the War of
Independence, and although officially over at this point there
were still pockets of resistance around the country.

In the 1930s the issue was trespass. Several men were brought
to court owing to what was claimed to be a 'tremendous
amount of trespass'. The defendants were listed as Thomas
Dempsey, Campile; Patrick Carew, Ferrybank; Patrick Cashin,
Drumdowney; John Black and Richard Atkins of Glasshouse;
and Cheekpoint men Denis Hennebry and Michael Heffernan.
The solicitor representing the railway stated that the men were
putting their own lives at risk by travelling the line either by

foot or bicycle. The case against Mikey Heffernan was struck out, and Atkins' hearing was adjourned. The others faced a fine of 6*d* and costs amounting to 7*s*.[80]

At the outbreak of the Second World War, and for several months after, the bridge continued to see daily use. Irish citizens, those with Irish relatives and some refugees, fled the looming war. Many travellers could only find standing room on the decks of the ferry boats, and seating was a luxury on the train, too.[81] As the war wore on and shortages deepened, rail traffic was suspended due to a lack of coal. Regular services were only reinstated after the war.

My mother, like so many others, left for England in the 1950s. (She initially left on the *Great Western* – see following chapter – which discontinued passenger services in 1959). To her the bridge brought mixed emotions, sadness on leaving, fires burning in the village, the last farewell to the emigrants that would keep families fed. Of course, it was also of gladness when she would get to return across it for the following Christmas and it would give her the first view of home.

There were several shipping collisions in later years, too. My father always said that the only surprise about hitting the bridge was that there were not more. I remember hearing one as a child, where the stern of the ship was swept on to the central fender as it passed through, with minor damage to the ship and none to the bridge. The sound reverberated around the village like a clap of thunder.

On another occasion, 7 April 1986, the inbound Panamanian-registered ship MV *Balsa* struck and did considerable damage to the opening. She was 6,000 tonnes and was empty at the time (she was chartered to collect a cargo of malt), which may have contributed to the accident. The central span was damaged and the bridge was immediately closed to rail and shipping until an inspection was carried out.

The bridge strike that caused the most severe damage occurred on 7 March 1991. The MV *Amy*, a Dutch-registered coaster, again entering port, collided against the opening span of the bridge and knocked it out of line. The timber fenders and central wharf were also damaged. In fact, the damage was so severe that the railway line and shipping channels were immediately closed. However, legal writs started to fly as fourteen vessels were stranded in the port. Lawyers for the Port of New Ross and the ship owners and shipping companies must have had a field day.

Within days an agreement was reached to allow egress and entry via the undamaged side of the opening, but the railway line remained closed. It would be summer before the railway was again in use, saving rail passengers a bus transfer from Campile and a 40-mile round trip via New Ross. The repair was delayed as some suggested that the opening span be widened as part of the repair. I don't know if this was ever seriously costed, but when the original work was eventually put right it was reputed to have cost between 3 and 5 million Irish punts. The work was carried out by a Cobh salvage company, which operated from Cheekpoint. These lads are still remembered fondly in the village, renowned as much for their long hours of labour as their huge capacity for porter.

In its later years the mainstay of the line was the demands of the sugar beet factories that the Wexford farmers supplied so capably. From the late summer through to the winter I can vividly recall the length of the beet trains crossing over the bridge. We often stood to count them, marvelling that the engine had nearly entered the tunnel and the rolling stock was still coming on to the bridge from the Great Island side. However, change in agricultural and food industry practices was in the wind. The last of the factories closed in 2006 and with it the main business of the line.

With the end of the beet industry and the decline in passenger numbers, many fears were expressed for the viability of the line. Finally on Saturday, 18 September 2010, the last commercial train crossed over the Barrow Bridge,[82] ending the historic link created with its opening in 1906. A special event train was laid on for the occasion, proving at least that the train operator CIÉ had some sense of the historic nature of the decision.

Now there is talk of a greenway along the line to mirror the success of the Waterford greenway walking and cycling route. Others suggest that this vital piece of infrastructure be retained for use as a railway into the future. I honestly don't mind as long as some decision is taken that would ensure the bridge continues to operate and is not left to fall into decay. In an era of so much waste and planned obsolescence it's heartening to see something that was designed, and built, to last.

19

CAMPILE BOMBING

On the day following my father's ninth birthday, 26 August 1940, he witnessed something that profoundly marked his life. Up on the hills around the village he caught sight of his first ever German aeroplane, which was followed closely by the dropping of bombs on the small rural village of Campile, Co. Wexford, directly across from Cheekpoint, in which three young women lost their lives.

The Second World War years in Ireland, or 'the Emergency', were a time of rationing, hunger and a certain amount of fear, at least initially. The threat of invasion was real from either warring side, and from villages like Cheekpoint, sailors risked their lives to keep meagre supply lines open to both Britain and Ireland at extreme risk to themselves, some paying the ultimate price. For example, a neighbour of ours, Philip Hanlon, died four days later (30 August 1940) when the ship he was aboard was torpedoed.[83] My grandfather, Andy, served throughout the war as a crewman on a small coaster and the risks were obvious and foremost in seafaring families' lives.

On that day, Monday, 26 August, my father climbed up out of the village with his friend Jim (Dips) Doherty. They were going to set snares for rabbits in the hope of extra food at home. It was a bright clear morning with patchy cloud and a warm sun. The hill fields, which were between the village and the Minaun, afforded a brilliant view of not just the meeting of the three sister rivers at Cheekpoint, but of the harbour and the land stretching away to the sea, Waterford on their side, the neighbouring county of Wexford on the other.

Whilst ducking in and out of the furze-shrouded ditches where rabbit runs were more obvious, their youthful ears picked up an unfamiliar sound. Glancing around, they spied the dark green plane (it would later be confirmed as a Heinkel He 111), and as they watched it came up the Wexford side of the river towards Nuke and then along the shoreline to Dunbrody and the main Waterford–Rosslare railway line. It then continued towards Slieve Coillte and turned in an arc towards the Barrow Bridge. Descending as it went, it proceeded to follow the railway line. It was only flying at a few hundred feet as it came in over the small railway station and rural village at Campile, and then out of the bottom of the plane dropped three bombs in quick succession.[84]

Their mouths fell open in fear and excitement and, as they instinctively ran for the village, I'm sure their minds were filled with panic and dread. Jim's mother was from the Wexford side and my father had relations there, too. They heard the sound of the bombs detonating rather than saw them. It was later that the boys heard that the plane had turned around and made a second run.

Arriving home, my father found the house empty, but proceeding down to the quay he found the area ablaze with activity. Already boats had left for Campile Pill and Great Island, and others were getting ready. He tried to tell what he had seen, but all the adults were fully aware, and their thoughts now were with their near neighbours, and in some cases family. There was more than one person in tears.

It was late that night before the grim news was brought back to the village. In a direct hit on the farming co-operative, three young women were dead and parts of the village had been on fire and lay in ruin. The death toll was considered miraculously low. For example, a fair had been on earlier in the morning but had finished prior to the raid. And many of the staff of the co-operative had gone home for lunch or were sitting outside the building enjoying the sunshine. Army, guards and volunteers alike had spent the evening clearing the rubble, ensuring that everyone was accounted for.[85] There had also been an unexploded bomb to deal with.

The funerals were massive and the event was widely reported, while people came from as far away as Belfast to view the scene. At the inquiry afterwards, various opinions were expressed as to why it had occurred and indeed some eyewitnesses claimed that the plane had come over the Minaun and had turned at the Barrow Bridge. As my father explained it, it was all a matter of where you viewed it from.

As for the reason for the bombing, the most prevalent account is that allied soldiers had been captured on the Continent and butter from the co-op was identified in their supplies, and thus it became a legitimate target. However, the official inquest found that both the co-operative and the supplies that travelled on the South West Wexford railway line were the actual targets. (A lesser-known event that day was that another Heinkel He 111 had bombed a viaduct further along the railway line.)

Of course, some people hold the view that it was all a big mistake. The one time I saw my father really upset about the event was when we were attending a wedding in Waterford's Tower Hotel. There was a chap in our company who put forward the opinion that the airmen thought they were over England or Wales. My father was less than civil about the matter. He pointed out that the day was so fine they could have been in no doubt where they were. He also explained that they followed the coast and the train tracks like reading a map. His final point, however, silenced all further discussion on the matter.

If the Luftwaffe thought they were in Wales or England, why did they descend to a few hundred feet to drop their bombs? They would have dropped them from a height where they would have a fighting chance of surviving a ground barrage from the air defences spread all over the British countryside. The only reason they came so low, he pointed out, was that they knew there was nothing to shoot at them from the ground, and they were bombing a defenceless neutral.

In recent years I published a blog on the topic and was amazed at the reaction it received. What was most interesting to me were the dozens of comments from people who remembered their parents talking about the event as children like my father; where they were that day, what they saw, what they did. It was an event that left a massive scar on the communities in the area, most particularly on the small rural community of Campile. I suppose it shattered my father's innocence that day. Gone was any thought that war was far away, and it probably served to underline the risks his father and others were enduring at sea.

If you are anywhere near Campile village in the future, why not drop by? Take a moment at the recently created memorial garden and try to imagine the shock and trauma visited upon this rural idyll, relatively not so very long ago.

An excellent source of information on the tragedy is *The Campile Bombing, August 26th, 1940* (2010) published by Horeswood Historical Society, Wexford.

20

THE *GREAT WESTERN*

By the virtue of how we spoke about ships in our community growing up, they almost assumed human characteristics. They were always a she, always had qualities that you might associate with the feminine, and the favourites were almost universally described in very affectionate terms.

Those that stood out included a workboat called the *Knocknagow*, the dredger known as the *Portlairge* and cross-channel boats such as the *Tuskar* or the *Rockabill*. But the queen of them all, at least in my eyes, was the *Great Western*. As my mother grew up it was this ship that passed her window so regularly and it was aboard her that she had travelled to England to work in those hungry years of the 1950s. The ship herself was owned by the Great Western Railway Company and ran from the Adelphi Quay in Waterford city (on the quay beside the present Tower Hotel) first to Milford Haven in Wales and later to Fishguard.

Of course, there was another reason the *Great Western* and ships like her were highly thought of – employment. In those days when the harbour villages were populated by seafarers, local work was a rarity. Most men had to travel abroad to get a ship, and deep sea voyages could mean absences of months or even years from home. Half a month's pay was generally sent home to the family; the other half was paid off, less expenses or pocket money, once a journey was over. This put a huge financial strain on families, but it was probably the emotional strain of the absence that was felt most. A job on the Irish Sea boats meant a regular income, and at least a somewhat normal home life. It was also a handy start for young lads wanting to make the sea their livelihood.

I think the fondness for the *Great Western*, or its familiarity, was that there were actually three vessels that shared the name and operated from Waterford. The first *Great Western* (1867–90) was a paddle steamer, while the next (1902–33) was a twin-screw steamer that operated on the route until 1933. This was replaced by a third *Great Western* (1933–66).

In 1923 a curious incident befell the second ship as she passed down the river close to Cheekpoint. From the Kilkenny shore, in the trees of Drumdowney, shots were fired into the ship narrowly missing the wireless operator named Daly and Captain Owen, who was standing on the bridge. No motive was discovered for the affair.

A passenger with a literary turn of phrase captured the departure at the very same point a few years later, but this time it was to describe a shower of love, rather than bullets!

I stood in the shelter of the bridge of the SS Great Western on a warm, showery Saturday afternoon early in September … Perched on a deck raft a freckled, Titian-haired girl scanned the river bank as we approached Cheekpoint. There was a searching look of farewell in her eyes. And then as the riverside hamlet at the foot of the Minaun hove in sight a white handkerchief fluttered from her hand. From every doorway there was an answering response. Away in the

distance little groups outside isolated whitewashed cottages
signalled to her their parting greetings. Young people on the
quay gesticulated, and children ran among the trees and along
the path bordering the river shrieking their good-byes. Two
prawngs (prongs), boats with high, curved prows peculiar to
the Passage and Cheekpoint fishermen, were almost mid-
stream, and young men stood up and waved their caps to the
girl on the deck raft. There were tears in the girl's eyes as the
scene faded away and the Great Western rounded another
bend of the Suir and nosed her way past Passage, Duncannon
Fort, Woodstown and the Hook lighthouse to the smooth,
open sea in the gathering dusk ...[86]

A few years later the third and final ship commenced on
the Waterford–Fishguard route in January 1934. Built by
the Cammell Laird shipyard in Birkenhead in 1933, she was
another twin-screw steamer that was 283ft long and 40ft wide,
of 1,659 tons and with a top speed of 14 knots. She could
accommodate 250 first-class and 200 third-class passengers,[87]
but she was principally a cargo boat for carrying livestock and
it was regularly remarked that the cattle or other animals were
first to be embarked when she arrived into port.

She didn't get off to a great start, for only a month after
her maiden voyage she grounded in thick fog in an effort to
avoid another craft:

It was then that a swift current caught her stern and carried
her on to the bank, where she had to remain until the next
tide to be re-floated. With extreme difficulty she made the
trip to Fishguard, where she was examined by the company's
diver last Monday. On the result of the examination it was

found necessary that she should be sent back to her builders in Liverpool for repairs to her stern. Until her repairs are completed she will be replaced by the Ardmore.[88]

The route was expanded in 1939 to three sailings a week, commencing with a 7 p.m. sailing on Monday, 6 March.[89] During the Second World War she was painted in camou- flage and later guns were added to her forward deck, manned by a naval gun crew. Although I have heard people say she was involved in the evacuation of Dunkirk, I have never as yet proved it. She did serve as a troop transporter for a time and late in the war she was allocated a destroyer and motor gunboat escort due to fears of U-boat attack.[90]

In February 1947, the local papers announced that the *Great Western* was being converted to an oil-burning engine and that the accommodation for passengers and crew was being extended, rearranged and generally improved.[91]

The ship herself was reported as carrying everything from emigrants, holidaymakers, cattle, horses, sheep, pigs and goats, and even cars were imported on her decks. Not everything being carried was legitimate, of course, and in post-war Britain, where shortages continued for many more years, the temptation of passengers to board with extra supplies was too great at times, as commented on in the local press:

Having a good time in Eire is one thing, but carrying away surreptitiously quantities of butter, bacon, cigarettes and chocolates is another aspect of tourism not so delightful to the natives. The customs 'swoop' in Waterford Tuesday, when the passengers' luggage on the SS Great Western was minutely scrutinised, revealed the extent of this smuggling traffic. It seems all-too-human, for the temptation to bring food home out of a land that seems to be abundantly supplied, to a country faced with dire austerity, is almost irresistible. It is hard to blame our British visitors, who have suffered the terrible strain and tragedy of six years of war and who are reduced to a bare subsistence, for what individually appear to be small evasions of our customs regulations. One report says it is estimated that the butter taken off passengers on the SS Great Western at Adelphi Quay, Waterford, on Tuesday, in varying lots totalled some 30 lbs. When we remember that the weekly ration of butter in Eire for the natives is 4 oz. we also realise how illusory is the present luxury in the hotels.[92]

Emigration was a primary reason people travelled on the vessel and this report from one week in August 1949 gives a clear idea of the numbers:

Cross-Channel Visitors. Seven hundred and seventy-seven visitors – 232 more than arrived – returned to England during last week on the SS Great Western sailing to Fishguard. On the outward journey the vessel carried 274 on Tuesday, 203 on Thursday, and conveyed about 300 Saturday evening. She brought 189 in Tuesday, Thursday and 261 on Saturday morning.[93]

My mother emigrated from Ireland in the autumn of 1958. She went to England in the company of Bob and Mary McDermott and their family. Bob, a Scotsman, was a marine engineer who sailed deep sea, and Mary was a Doyle, her mother originally hailing from the Russianside. My mother found work in homes, shops and eventually a factory job in the Trebor sweets plant in East London. She sailed back and forth regularly but as the passenger route was discontinued in 1959, she would thereafter take the Rosslare route.

She often speaks about those journeys and the crowds that went abroad to work. Her companions read like an address book of the village: her uncle, Christy Moran, heading to London to work on the buildings; Pat Murphy, Patsy Moran, Charlie Hanlon and many more heading to Wolverhampton; Michael Elliott, Andy Joe Doherty, Anna Sullivan and so on. All heading away to work and sending vital money home. She also recalled some great social occasions such as meeting Joan Brosnans (originally Joan Sullivan of Coolbunnia), who had a lodging house in Kilburn and how on a Saturday night she would meet up with others from the area and go dancing together.

Another memory was less happy. Her Uncle Michael had fallen from scaffolding and fractured his skull. He lingered for almost a month before he finally died. On awakening one morning she found the house in darkness, the mirrors covered and the women preparing for his wake. She remembers chancing to peek through the closed curtains at home that morning as the *Great Western* passed up the river. Her flag was at half-mast and she remembers it being black (as a consequence of the sun being behind it no doubt). Accompanying the coffin was her grandfather, Michael, who had been with his son when he finally died.

I think the most poignant story I know of is the leaving of the Condon family from the village in 1955. The 1950s were a hungry and bleak time nationally – so much so it has been described as a black decade, or a lost decade.

Chris Condon recently recalled the leaving to me. His dad, Christy, had invested in new nets to fish in 1954 but even the fish seemed to have deserted the country. Christy chose the boat to England, but he left his wife May and his eight children at home.

Christy was set up in a job by his brother, Liam. Liam had come in from a cold, wet and fruitless night of fishing with my grandfather (Andy Doherty) in 1946 and spotted an advertisement in a local paper for a new engineering firm, British Timken in Northampton. He was interviewed in a hotel in Waterford and was given the job on the spot. He was foreman by the 1950s and he helped Christy find his feet in the same company. With the job Christy kept the family fed in Cheekpoint and earned enough to put a deposit on a home.

In the summer of 1955 Christy returned to Cheekpoint to gather his family. They were an integral part of the village community, went to school, to mass, played on the village green, and swam off the village quay. Steps of stairs, they were part of the vitality of the community. The decision to leave was a huge wrench. But as big as it was for the family, it was often those who were left behind that felt it more, and their loss out of the village was profound.

The evening they sailed down from Waterford on the *Great Western* the village turned out to wave them away. Fires were lit from the Rookery to the Mount Quay and their cousins, the Rogers family, lit a fire at Passage East. Another local, Tom Sullivan, told me that he was a deckhand on her that evening and he overheard one person saying that if only she would sink now passing the village, the children could swim ashore and never have to leave. Mary Chaytor *née* Rogers told me recently that she was one of the Rogers family standing on the strand in Passage with the bonfire and watching the ship sail down. Her cousin, John Condon, who was 13 at the time, had said to her that when he passed the Spider Lighthouse and saw the bonfire he would whistle. He did so, and clear as a bell they heard it, their last link to their cousins until they returned on holidays the following year.

Many came home for their annual holiday, something that a good paying job abroad allowed. Recently Eiblis Howlett shared a memory with me of coming up the Suir with her siblings and father in the early morning. Eiblis recalled her father gazing out on his home city and reciting the following lines: 'O, Ireland! Isn't grand you look. Like a bride in her rich adornin. With all the pent up love of my heart. I bid you the top of the morning.'

The lines are from the poem 'The Exiles Return', or 'Morning on the Irish Coast', and were written by another exile, John Locke (1847–89). Locke was an Irish writer and Fenian activist, exiled to the United States. Unlike Eiblis and her family, however, Locke never did get to return.

For some, however, the journey home was part of a foreign schooling commute, such as the Waterford historian Julian Walton. Julian wrote about his trip home from school in England during the 1950s:

> But though her passengers were few, they felt themselves to be an honoured bunch. For the Great Western was a thorough lady. She departed at civilised hours and she took you straight to destination, unlike the wretched St David, which dumped you on the quayside at Rosslare in the freezing dark and left you to fight for a train seat. Staff and regular passengers knew

each other well. My friends the Anderson children persuaded the captain to sound the ship's siren when passing their house (Ballycar in Newtown) so that their mother would know it was time to head to town to collect them.[94]

The last trip of the *Great Western* was at Christmas 1966. In her illustrious wake came container ships; a freight system that would become the backbone of shipping in the city for the next few decades until the closure of Bell Lines in 1997. She brought an end to a proud shipping tradition in the area. The *Great Western* went to the breakers yard in Belgium the following year, a sad end to a terrific servant, but her name and reputation still resonates for many locals and emigrants around the globe.

21

OCEAN COAST RESCUE

I remember being curious about a framed certificate on the wall of the living room of our family home. It was for a rescue in the River Mersey in Liverpool and had my father's name on it. He would never say anything about it when I was growing up; he would, in fact, divert any questions away. It was one of those things he just chose not to speak about, but which I struggled to piece together in the years after he died.

He had gone to sea a bit later than most, as his father decided to ensure he completed a secondary education. His first ship was the MV *Cairngorm*, which he joined along with his father on 30 May 1951 in Waterford. On Saturday night, 12 November 1955, he was aboard the MV *Ocean Coast* as she departed Liverpool in dense fog bound for Falmouth.[95] The ship was carrying general cargo and with him that night was his younger brother, John, and a cousin from the village, Jimmy (O'Dea) Doherty.

Their ship was a twin-screw motor cargo vessel, 250ft in length with a 38ft beam and 1,790 tons dead weight. She was built for short sea route trips by Leith shipyard for the Coast Lines shipping company of Liverpool and was launched on 31 July 1935. During the war years she had served as a supply vessel to Gibraltar and North Africa. She also played her part in the D-Day landings servicing Omaha beach carrying petrol.

The first official communication on the night was at 22:10 when the *Ocean Coast* sent out the following message: 'Queens Channel, Q15 Buoy, River Mersey. There has been a collision between two unknown ships. I am anchored and sending a lifeboat over. Strong ebb tide running. One of the ships in the collision has sunk.'

The collision, it would subsequently emerge, involved a fully laden Swedish oil tanker SS *Juno*, which was inbound, and the SS *Bannprince*, which was operated by S. William Coe of Liverpool. The *Bannprince* had a crew of predominantly Northern Ireland men that night and had been built in 1933 in Glasgow. She was just over 165ft long with a beam of 27ft and a dead weight of 716 tons.

Like the *Ocean Coast*, the *Bannprince* had served with a volunteer crew during the war. She helped to evacuate 337,130 allied troops from Dunkirk between May and June 1940. Following this she was taken over for 'unspecified special government services' and was one of the first ships to land at Sword beach during the D-Day landings carrying much-needed medical supplies.

The *Bannprince* was outward bound that fateful night, fully laden with coal, for Coleraine in Northern Ireland. The first her crew knew of difficulties was when the ship's horn sounded three shrill blasts moments before there was an almighty crash and the ship heeled over. She would sink in ten minutes and most of the crew of nine had no time to get a life jacket. Her lifeboats were submerged. In the freezing Mersey the crew did what they could to stay together and help those that couldn't swim into life jackets found floating around on the surface or by holding on to other debris that would sustain them. The *Juno* was entering the Mersey and heading for the Liverpool docks.

The *Ocean Coast* was also struck by the tanker and one of her lifeboats was damaged in the collision. Luckily the other lifeboat was undamaged and this was subsequently launched and used in the search for survivors. At this point most of the sailors were close to exhaustion and had drifted apart, but the boat my father and Jimmy O'Dea was in rescued six, and a life-boat from a sister ship, *Southern Coast*, picked up the remaining three men including the captain and the only crewman to lose his life, second engineer James Ferris of Limavady, Derry.

They put the six survivors aboard the New Brighton life-boat and returned to the *Ocean Coast*, which turned back to port to replace the damaged lifeboat. On 3 April 1957, my father, along with five other crewmen (including Jimmy) received a certificate from the Liverpool Shipwreck and Humane Society in recognition of their efforts. The captain received a silver cigarette box and the chief officer a parch-ment. Unfortunately, it appears that neither my father's name nor any of the other crew was ever recorded in the papers, unlike the captains of both Coast Lines ships.[96]

The *Ocean Coast* continued to give service into the 1960s, when she seems to have been sold for scrap. The *Bannprince* was raised from the Mersey as she was a hazard to shipping and was sold for scrap to a Dutch shipyard.[97] The *Juno*, which was only lightly damaged, returned to work, but I couldn't source any further information about her.

My father's cousin and crewmate Jimmy O'Dea was also recognised after the rescue. Jimmy, of course, was a renowned teller of tall tales, so much so that if he said it was sunny out-side you'd be best to bring an umbrella. He had no reticence about talking about that night. According to him, when they approached the men in the water my father, who was an excellent swimmer, had to jump overboard to help some of the weakened men. When they had all the shipwrecked seamen aboard they headed back to their ship, but quickly noticed my father wasn't aboard. They turned back, rowing now with a vengeance only to find my father swinging off a buoy shouting, 'Where the hell were ye then shipmates?' Fact or fiction we'll never know, but my father would have loved it; the bigger the laugh the better, even at his own expense.

22

Remembering the 'Mud Boat' SS *Portlairge*

There are few more mundane yet vital services in any port than dredging. The job itself is to keep the mud and silt that gathers in check by digging it out of places where it interferes with the access to wharves, jetties and quays, and depositing it somewhere that it can do no further harm. You would think that a job so routine and mundane would go largely unnoticed in a busy port city such as Waterford, but the local dredger that was named after the Gaelic name of the city was the total opposite. She was the *Portlairge*, or to many simply 'the mud boat', and to generations her funnel smoke, boat's whistle and the rattling chains embodied the maritime tradition of the city.

As the port of Waterford developed in the nineteenth century, mud and its management was an issue for the harbour commissioners. The first mention I have found of a dredging machine dates to 1839,[98] and the system seems to have been a mechanical steel vessel that dredged up spoil and deposited it into flat-bottomed wooden barges. These barges were known locally as lighters. The lighters would then carry the mud away. In some cases it was used as fertiliser on fields, in other cases it helped to fill in behind embankments of reclaimed land or was simply dumped out of harm's way. In 1896 two men with the lofty title of 'Inspector of Mud Boats' were in trouble with the commissioners for dereliction of duties. Apparently the 'mud checkers were neglecting their business ...' and were not ensuring its proper disposal.[99]

The decision of the commissioners to invest not just in a new dredger, but a technologically advanced one, led to the awarding of a contract to the Liffey Dock Yard Company based in Dublin. In July 1907, the tug *Knight Errant* towed this new dredger from Dublin to Glasgow, where her steam engines were to be fitted.[100] The following month the commissioners decided that the wife of their secretary, one Mrs John Allingham, would be the sponsor at the naming ceremony of what was decided to be called the *Portlairge,* in Dublin. The position of captain was also decided at the same meeting, at least on a trial basis. The honour went to Vincent Martin, who had served in the two previous dredgers, *Urbs Intacta* and *Sicily.*[101]

The vessel got several write-ups in the local papers to acknowledge her arrival in port. The *Waterford Chronicle*[102] gave a very thorough account of her specifications:

> The dimensions of the vessel are B.P. 140 feet by 29 feet beam by 12 feet. 6 inches moulded depth and she is capable of carrying 500 tons of spoil when floating at her load draught of 11 ft. She is built of steel to the highest class at Lloyd's, and under their special survey, and has additional strengthening on the bottom and other important parts where experience has

proved such be necessary. Of the flush deck type she is well subdivided; having no less than ten watertight compartments, and is practically unsinkable.[103] The propelling machinery is placed aft, and in order that the vessel may steam well when light in bad weather a large trimming tank is fitted forward having capacity of 60 tons, and the tank is capable of being emptied by the engine room pumps in about 30 minutes … Accommodation is fitted forward in the vessel for the crew, and in the water-tight compartment immediately abaft of this is a neat saloon tastefully done up in polished hardwoods, with comfortable accommodation for the captain and officers in cabins adjoining.

Both Allingham and William Friel[104] were aboard for the journey from Dublin on Tuesday, 10 September. A brief report of the journey was conveyed in the *Munster Express*,[105] where we learn that the harbour master, Captain Farrell, was in charge and he states, 'she travelled splendidly at the rate of 9½ knots per hour against wind and rain'. There were many visitors to inspect the new dredger, but as behoves a work-boat, there was no time lost in getting down to duty and the report concludes that, 'She worked in a very satisfactory manner all day on Thursday.'

The duties of the crew in later years were described by Sonny Condon.[106] She had then a crew complement of captain, mate, engineer, fireman, two crane drivers and two deck hands. She was docked at the London Hulk (opposite Reginald's Tower) and the first man aboard for each day's work was the fireman (in my times this was a fellow Cheekpoint man, Billy 'Dips' Doherty). The fireman got the fire going in the boiler to prepare for the day's work.

The crew boarded at 8 a.m. and the vessel steamed to the location requiring dredging. Once her holds were full she would come back to her mooring for lunch and in the early afternoon head away to dump the load. She would steam out as far as the Hook in later years (she had used the King's Channel for some time) and as the holds were opened and the spoil was dropped, she would pop up out of the water, close her hold doors, and then turn for home. On regaining the quay, the boiler and furnace were shut down and the second furnace was prepared for the following day.

In my youth the men I associated with the *Portlairge* were those who probably served out their time on it, and these included Michael Heffernan, who was the skipper; Billy Doherty, who I already mentioned; Charlie 'Wag' Duffin and Jimmy Condon – all of whom came from Cheekpoint or were originally from there. John Donnelly was from Passage East and the engineer was Jacques and from the city.

There were some great times had with the crew and it was often I would chat with Charlie Duffin when I was on my own lunch from De La Salle in the late 1970s and early '80s. The belching smoke from her funnel reminded me of a warm and cosy fireside; the conditions were often the total opposite on Waterford's quays in midwinter.

A follower of my blog who now resides in America[107] passed along some fond memories of the ship and her crew; his father was Jacques the engineer. Paul had the pleasure of doing a shift on the *Portlairge* with his father one Saturday morning. There were two to three hours of dredging at the Clyde Wharf, after which they steamed down river, but 'hove to' close to Waterpark College. The small punt that was used as the ship's tender slipped away with two of the lads aboard and ranged a 'scooneen' (a short fishing net secured in place from the riverbank), which they had set previously. When they returned they had two salmon, which were carefully taken aboard. They then steamed out to the Hook to dump the spoil and then back up the river, where they dropped anchor outside Passage. Then it was into the punt and off to Twomey's bar to trade fish for beer. Paul was sworn to secrecy as they were on overtime and obviously poaching salmon or drinking on the job was a no-no.

Salmon wasn't the only fish I associated with the dredger, of course. They often gathered up large quantities of eel that were sleeping in the mud that was dredged. As the bucket came in over the side, the eels would drop and squirm all over the decks. Crewmen who were fast on their feet and dexterous with their hands could scoop up a few stone of eels before they slithered out of the combings. There was a ready market for the catch, perhaps the most popular being the European ships berthed on the city quays.

Unfortunately another 'catch' in the bucket at times were dead bodies; in fact, I've read four different accounts from only a very brief examination of the papers. One incident concerned Big Patsy Doherty, who featured in our account of the *Alfred D Snow*. Patsy was a winchman on her when he lifted a body up in the bucket at the Liverpool hulk in 1953. Called on to give evidence at a subsequent inquest, Patsy's knowledge of the river was called on: 'The water was between 18 to 20 feet at that point, and from my knowledge of the flow of the tide I would say the body entered at about that point …' The body was identified as John Breddy from Cork; he was employed as a land steward at Prospect House.[108]

Of course, as befitted a workboat, the dredger performed a variety of other tasks around the port and harbour. She was built with several purposes in mind and this included helping with navigation buoy maintenance, towage and salvage. For example, in November 1954[109] she towed off the *SS City of Cork* when she grounded coming up the river near the King's Channel on soft mud. Her crew attached a rope and on the high water towed the vessel safely off without incident. The undamaged *City of Cork* then proceeded into port under her own steam.

Eddie Fardy, of Rathfadden Villas in the city, was telling me recently that he signed on as relief crew on the *Portlairge* in the 1970s. He was part of the shore gang but when an opportunity arose he jumped at the chance to join her, as there was more money when afloat. Eddie was down below mostly and recalled how water frequently dripped off the pipes and scalded your head and neck. Cloth was used to seal up any drips, but that was cold comfort if boiling water dripped into your ear!

Charlie Duffin popped down to him one day when they were heading out the harbour and suggested Eddie could take a turn on deck. Eddie was delighted to get out of the heat but on stepping out on deck he nearly perished with the cold. He was starting to realise his mistake when he was accosted by another crewman who challenged his right to be there. Eddie explained himself and was told to 'report back to the engine room' and get Charlie back on deck where he was required. Eddie was delighted to go back into the heat, and all Charlie did was laugh and wink at him. He wasn't known as 'The Wag' Duffin for nothing.

The end of the *Portlairge* is still very contentious and the contemporary local and national newspapers were filled with claims and counter-claims. Although I lived through the era, I have to admit I found it difficult to follow. Here's what I could decipher from the accounts.

In my final year at school it was reported[110] that the *Portlairge* was no longer able to perform her duties. She had broken down in late 1982 and the contemporary situation was described thus: 'The old ship, which is the oldest coal-fired working steam vessel afloat, is older than most people in Waterford and it is regarded with great affection by young and old. One of the two steam-driven cranes and buckets on the ship has broken down and she can no longer keep the berths free of mud …' The Harbour Board was to maintain dredging with her to June, at which point she was due her annual inspection.

The affection in which she was held had led to previous calls that she be preserved and turned into a museum piece. The local branch of An Taisce had tried this in 1980 but in a report at the time their approaches had not been well received and the Harbour Board's response to them was described as 'most discourteous and unhelpful in their efforts to preserve the boat …' However, it was also reported that 'the Commissioners said they would help them in every way possible to get the boat but they would not provide any money …'[111] It would appear there were also fears that the Board would be expected to appoint a watchman over the vessel.

At some point in late 1983 or early 1984 the sale of the *Portlairge* was agreed with Treloar Brothers of Northumberland for £3,500 but local objections were raised and a counterbid was offered. However as a contract had been signed the Board did not think they could go back on the original agreement.[112] The dredger was securely moored at the Scotch Quay in Johns Pill at this stage.

In 1986 the *Irish Independent* covered the story of her sale.[113] Although still at the Scotch Quay in a peaceful backwater, the vessel herself was at the centre of a heated dispute. The local bid by conservationists had, it was claimed, scared off the Northumberland investors. (I think it fair to say the Treloar Brothers had the skill to at least preserve the ship, although I think the operation has since ceased.) As a consequence, the vessel had since been resold to a Wexford man named Sean Finn, who was described as a garage owner from New Ross. Finn, it was reported, had plans to move the ship to Fethard-on-Sea with the intention of keeping her as a working vessel and a tourist attraction.

The story continued to rumble on and locally I recall that many were of the opinion that the ship was so identified with the city that she could never be allowed to leave. However, others were concerned about the costs of both keeping and then refurbishing the boat. In the Ireland of the 1980s, when economic recession was an acute reality, where would a city such as Waterford find the cash? In my youthful enthusiasm I wondered should we not take direct action, board her, claim her as our own and refuse to allow her to leave? Silly perhaps, but in hindsight I wish I had; at least I could say I had tried to do something.

Eventually, on Wednesday, 26 August 1987, the *Portlairge* departed her city. She was weeks away from her eightieth birthday and had served us faithfully for seventy-seven years. The *Cork Examiner* claimed that she sailed away almost unnoticed.[114] I would dispute that claim and suggest that never was a more inaccurate line written.

She now sits a total ruin on a mudflat in Saltmills in Co. Wexford. Whatever plans the new owner had for her, this was hardly what he had in mind. No one could say this is where she belongs or what they would want for such a boat, but stripped of all her value she corrodes into the element that she once so valiantly controlled. Many have said she should be purchased (if she would be sold!) and returned. I fear it's now neither practical nor feasible.

I visit her now probably once a year, and it's rare that I am alone. It seems that many make a regular pilgrimage to the mud boat, but we are like mourners visiting a graveyard, silent, reserved and introspective. I wonder if like me they remember her in her heyday, her indomitable crew, the rattle of her chains as she worked and the taunts of the smart young lads on the quays as she departed downriver – 'bring us back a parrot'.

23

RAMBLING OVER THE MINAUN

And so we come to the end, and I return to my childhood. One of the most beautiful views, and quieter walks, that you will find in County Waterford is the Minaun. The hilltop overlooks the meeting of the three sister rivers (Barrow, Nore and Suir) at Cheekpoint and with panoramas over the counties of the south-east, down the harbour and out to the Saltee Islands.

The Minaun was one of our favourite playgrounds as children, particularly on Sunday afternoon walks with our mother. There we ran wild and there were several spots that were favourites. My own was the round piece of stone, where local tradition had it the Knights of the Round Table met. (It was actually the remains of an old mill stone quarrying operation.) We would play at King Arthur with pretend swords and shields and talk like the actors such as Robert Taylor, familiar to us from the black and white movies on RTÉ Television. Another rock feature was shaped like a loaf of bread, or other times we called it a grave, holding one of the knights that had fallen in battle.

One of the best views in those days was on the rock outcrop on the top, a favourite place for picnics. There you could see a curious decaying rectangular-shaped stump of timber cemented into place. It marked the remains of a religious cross that was erected in 1950 in conjunction with a Holy Year announced by Pope Pius XII. According to my mother, her uncle, Christy Moran, and his wife (the driving force) Katie *née* Doherty, had asked a local craftsman, named Chris Sullivan, to make the cross. To pay for it, Katie went door to door in the community and although people had little enough, they paid what they could, perhaps because they were a little afraid of her. Katie, after all, had a reputation for religious fervour.

My father, of course, had a different take on it. He agreed with the basics of my mother's account, but then diverted with dramatic effect; for he was one of the unfortunates who was appointed by Katie to get the completed cross on to the summit.

As he told it, the boys of the area had been rounded up by Katie and no excuses would be heard. At an appointed hour they met at Chris' in Coolbunnia. Most of the village had turned out and there was a festive atmosphere. Katie had the boys hoist the cross on to their backs and then encouraged and cajoled them up the road from Coolbunnia to where the present National School stands, and then up onto the Minaun's summit. As they went Katie played her melodeon box and sang religious hymns. My father often joked that the only difference between themselves and Jesus was that Katie spared them the whip and the crown of thorns.

As they slipped and fell on the way to the summit, Katie interrupted the musical programme to shout encouragements and threats. By the time they reached the summit, or

Golgotha as he called it, they were cut and bruised and had she nailed my father to the cross itself, he wouldn't have had the energy to prevent it.

My mother claimed the cross was not all that heavy and that they only fell three times to blackguard Katie! Once erected, the cross was blessed by Reverend Murphy, Chaplin to the De La Salle novitiate at Faithlegg, and thereafter it symbolised to some the Holy Year called by the Pope, but for many it was, as it had always been, a lovely spot for a picnic and a view.

Today the cross is only a memory; the timber has completely rotted away, although the rectangular outline of the shaft remains. Many of the other features still remain, too. I was interested recently to read that, according to legend, the Fianna used the Minaun in their defence of Leinster and so important was it to their leader, Fionn Mac Cumhaill, that he deputised a son, Cainche Corcardhearg, to wait in watch as protector of his realm. Apparently he lives below the ground up there … lying in wait![115] He must be sleeping soundly … any number of invaders have swept past him in the intervening years.

Visitors to the summit were common. My mother told me that as a child she remembered 'townies' walking out to take the view on Sunday afternoons. I've read newspaper accounts from the nineteenth century of Sunday boating trips, coming down river from Waterford, mooring in the village and climbing to the Minaun to enjoy the panorama. Before returning home, the better-off took tea in the village or aboard their yachts and sailed back up on the incoming tide.

One of the earliest recorded visitors that I know of is Arthur Young, who stayed with local landlord Cornelius

Bolton in the eighteenth century. Young was an English writer on agriculture, economics and social statistics who visited the locality twice. He is arguably best known for his first-hand observations on the French Revolution of 1789.

His book, *Arthur Young's Tour in Ireland (1776–1779)*,[116] is filled with social, economic and political observations, and he gave amazing insights into the locality. He described the geography of the Minaun with great accuracy and declared that it was one of the best views that he saw in Ireland. He liked it so much in fact that he rode or walked to it daily.

During the era of the Power family (landlords of Faithlegg 1819–1936), the summit was given over to dense planting to create a fox covert, an area set aside for the protection of foxes. Protected, of course, is a loose term, as they were then chased by the local hunt, the Faithlegg Harriers, and the pack of hounds and their guests from across the county and beyond. In the 1960s the area was planted by the state forestry service, which perhaps protected the amenity somewhat, but ruined the view in later years. In the late 1970s a large satellite dish was sited there to provide UK TV to city dwellers, and in the '80s a round tower was built near the top. As ugly and out of place as you could ever imagine, this tower's purpose has always remained a mystery. Although the views are much diminished now, it remains a beautiful walk with some stunning aspects nonetheless.

When I go there now I'm often drawn back to my childhood games. And often too I laugh to myself on thinking of the stories of my father, and the mock disdain of his accounts by my mother. Between the two of them we had a very interesting storytelling process: my father with the dramatic and outrageous, my mother with the cautious and more grounded facts. I try to manage a balance between the two, accurate but still interesting.

Follow my blog, www.tidesandtales.ie, for more of these stories, or let me know what you thought of the book by emailing me at tidesntales@gmail.com.

NOTES

CHAPTER 1

1. *Waterford Chronicle*, Tuesday, 1 April 1777.
2. Hutchinson, J.R., *The Press Gang Afloat and Ashore*, 2010, Fireship Press.
3. *Cork Examiner*, 1 September 1883, p. 5 (a piece looking back on newspaper reports from 1770).

CHAPTER 2

4. The term Old or Oul IRA (Irish Republican Army) was often used by the men in the 1970s to differentiate between the early years of independence and the then campaign in Northern Ireland.
5. See for example John de Courcy Ireland's great work, *Ireland's Sea Fisheries: A History*, 1981, The Glendale Press, Dublin.
6. Colfer, B., *The Hook Peninsula*, 2004, Cork University Press, Cork, p. 62.
7. 'An actual survey of the harbour and river of Waterford, and the Bay of Tramore: with the adjacent coast, from Great Newtown Head to Bagenbon Head', Bernard Scale, 1787.
8. Colfer, B., *The Hook Peninsula*, 2004, Cork University Press, Cork, p. 30.

CHAPTER 3

9. Much of the detail is taken from *I Was a Day in Waterford* edited by T.N. Fewer from a piece by Julian Walton called 'Cornelius Bolton and the Packet Service', pp. 49–53.
10. Young, A., *A Tour in Ireland 1776–1779*, 1970, Irish University Press, Shannon.
11. Antell, R., *The Mails Between South West Wales and Southern Ireland: The Milford–Waterford Packet 1600–1850*, 2011, Welsh Philatelic Society, p. 19.
12. Ibid., pp. 19–20.
13. Ibid., p. 20.

14. Ibid., p. 20.
15. Ibid., p. 37.

CHAPTER 4

16. Much of the information throughout the chapter on the service and the *Ida* is drawn from an article written by Bill Irish in *Decies* No. 53 titled 'The Waterford Steamship Company', 1997, pp. 67–89. Also McRonald, M., *The Irish Boats Vol. 2. Liverpool to Cork and Waterford*, 2006, Tempus, Stroud, Gloucestershire.
17. From my own reading I think that the *Maid of Erin* and the *Repealer* were possibly one and the same.
18. Quoted from 'Jogging My Memory, The Monks School New Ross in the 1880s', Mark Canon O'Byrne. From *The Past: The organ of the Uí Cinsealaigh Historical Society*, No. 18, 1992, pp. 55–74.
19. *Tipperary Free Press*, Tuesday, 26 July 1870.

CHAPTER 5

20. See for example Roche, R., *Tales of the Wexford Coast*, 1993, Duffry Press, Enniscorthy.
21. *The Gentleman's Magazine* of 1766 gave details of the trial and the hanging of the four; George Gidley and Richard St Quintin both west of England men, Peter McKinlie, an Irishman, and Dutchman Andreas Zekerman (with thanks to Brian Forristal).

CHAPTER 6

22. A cot is a locally traditional boat of the upper waters, thought to have originated from log boats. Although not as common today, examples are still to be found around Carrick on Suir and New Ross.
23. For a description of the fishery, the weirs and their operation see my previous book, *Before the Tide Went Out*, 2017.
24. *Connaught Telegraph*, 17 July 1833, p. 4.
25. Maddock, Fidelma, *The Cot Fishermen of the River Nore*, pp. 541–565, Kilkenny History and Society, 1990, Geography Press (editors Nolan, W. and Whelan, K.).
26. Quoted in *Sliabh Rua: A History of its People and Places*, ed. Jim Walsh, 2001, p. 251.
27. *Freeman's Journal*, 3 April 1844, p.4.

CHAPTER 8

28. www.dippam.ac.uk/eppi/documents/9788/page/214351, accessed 4 May 2017.

29. Private correspondence with Paul O'Farrell, California, USA.
30. *The Cambrian*, 23 June 1932 (with thanks to Myles Courtney).
31. *Kerry Evening Post*, Saturday, 23 June 1832, p. 3.
32. The previous paragraphs mentioned a station employed at Passage East in 1828. This was either an error in official documentation or more likely a floating hospital was on station for a period of time, but was redeployed. These floating hospitals were sometimes referred to as lazarettos.
33. *Waterford Mirror*, Thursday, 18 December 1884.
34. *Waterford Standard*, Saturday, 5 June 1905.
35. *Waterford Standard*, Friday, 21 October 1910.
36. *Waterford Standard*, Saturday, 11 June 1949.

CHAPTER 9

37. *A Dictionary of the World's Watercraft*, The Mariners' Museum, 2000, Chatham Publishing.
38. *A Maritime History of Ringsend*, 2000, Sandymount Community Services.
39. Brophy, Anthony J., 'Port of Waterford. Extracts from the Records of the Waterford Harbour Commissioners from their Establishment in 1816 to the Report of the Ports and Harbours Tribunal 1930'. *Decies,* No. 60, pp.151–169.

CHAPTER 10

40. Smith, G., *King's Cutters. The Revenue Service and the War against Smuggling*, 1983, Conway Maritime Press, London.
41. Detailed Account of Establishment for Collection of Customs and Ports of Ireland 1821–22. Enhanced British Parliamentary Papers on Ireland Sourced from http://dippam.ac.uk/eppi/documents/9544/page2/210933 (1 September 2017).

CHAPTER 11

42. The map, or more correctly a chart, is called 'An actual survey of the harbour and river of Waterford, and of the Bay of Tramore: with the adjacent coast, from Great Newtown Head to Bagenbon Head'. Drawn by Bernard Scales in 1787. A high-resolution chart can be accessed online at: http://digitalarchive.mcmaster.ca/islandora/object/macrepo:21835
43. *Waterford News*, Friday, 16 February 1866, p. 3.
44. Account of Mitchell's life, www.historyireland.com/18th-19th-century-history/alexander-mitchell-1780-1868-belfasts-blind-engineer (accessed 1 February 2019).
45. *Waterford News*, 18 January 1867. With thanks to Charley McCarthy for the reference.

46. *Waterford Standard*, Saturday, 15 December 1894, p. 3.
47. *Waterford Standard*, Saturday, 19 October 1895, p. 3.
48. *New Ross Standard*, Friday, 26 June 1914, p. 3.

CHAPTER 12

49. *Irish Independent*, 8 September 1925.
50. *Donegal News*, 8 August 1931.
51. From a piece titled 'To earn a living under sail', *Yacht and Yachting Magazine*, 11 December 1964.
52. *Cork Examiner*, 9 January 1937.

CHAPTER 14

53. McElwee, R., *The Last Voyages of the Waterford Steamers*, 1992, The Book Centre, Waterford.
54. Ibid.
55. Babb, Anthony, *U-Boat Enigmas*, 2019, Amazon, UK.
56. Ibid.
57. Ibid.
58. From private email correspondence with Robin Richards (son of Commander Richards).
59. Nolan et al., *Secret Victory: Ireland and the War at Sea 1914–18*, 2009, Mercier Press, Cork.
60. Macintyre, D., *Fighting Under the sea*, 1965, Evan Brothers Ltd, London.
61. Babb, Anthony, *U-Boat Enigmas*, 2019, Amazon, UK.
62. Stokes, R., *Between the Tides: Shipwrecks of the Irish Coast*, 2015, Amberley, Gloucestershire.
63. Nolan et al., *Secret Victory. Ireland and the War at Sea 1914–18*, 2009, Mercier Press, Cork.
64. Stokes, R., *Between the Tides: Shipwrecks of the Irish Coast*, 2015, Amberley, Gloucestershire.
65. Ibid.
66. Email correspondence between the author and Nicki Kenny, originally from Germany, who had traced the information for a previous blog.
67. Stokes, R., *Between the Tides; Shipwrecks of the Irish Coast*, 2015, Amberley, Gloucestershire.

CHAPTER 15

68. Many of the details in this chapter come from the work of McElwee, R., *The Last Voyages of the Waterford Steamers*, 1992, The Book Centre, Waterford.
69. *Freeman's Journal*, Tuesday, 23 February 1915, p. 7.
70. Walton, J. & O'Donoghue, F., *On This Day* Vol. II, 2014.

CHAPTER 18

71. Shepherd, E., *Fishguard & Rosslare Railways & Harbour Company*, 2015, Colourpoint Books, Newtownards.
72. Ibid.
73. *Waterford Standard*, Saturday, 30 March 1946, p. 4.
74. Ibid.
75. Warping was a procedure that I referred to earlier in the hobbler story.
76. *New Ross Standard*, 3 March 1905, p. 7.
77. *Cork Examiner*, 26 July 1907.
78. Nolan et al., *Secret Victory. Ireland and the War at Sea 1914–18*, 2009, Mercier Press, Cork.
79. *Munster Express*, 9 June 1923.
80. *Munster Express*, 3 December 1937.
81. McShane, M., *Neutral Shores. Ireland and the Battle of the Atlantic*, 2012, Mercier Press, Cork.
82. *Irish Times*, Monday, 20 September 2010.

CHAPTER 19

83. SS *Mill Hill* (1930) was a Tynesider and was attacked on 30 August 1940 by *U-32* as part of convoy HX-66A 58 miles west north-west of Cape Wrath. All thirty-four crew aboard were lost and three other ships were lost in the same incident.
84. Cummins, Patrick J., *Emergency Air Incidents South East Ireland 1940–1945*, 2004, Aviation History Ireland, Waterford.
85. *Mid-Ulster Mail*, Saturday, 31 August 1940, p. 6.

CHAPTER 20

86. *Waterford Standard*, Saturday, 7 October 1933, p. 6.
87. Details accessed from www.doverferryphotosforums.co.uk/new-ts-great-western-iii1933-past-and-present/?fbclid=IwAR2OSG9Vidj2C yEY7vTnQMxoJNEC92y6ypFlOen4pmmTdGIBX9az22HeWwU, Saturday, 16 March 2019 via Frank Cheevers.
88. *Waterford Standard*, Saturday, 24 February 1934, p. 4.
89. *Waterford Standard*, Saturday, 11 March 1939, p. 7.
90. Details accessed from www.doverferryphotosforums.co.uk/new-ts-great-western-iii1933-past-and-present/?fbclid=IwAR2OSG9Vidj2C yEY7vTnQMxoJNEC92y6ypFlOen4pmmTdGIBX9az22HeWwU, Saturday, 16 March 2019 via Frank Cheevers.
91. *Waterford Standard*, Saturday 8 February 1947, p. 4.
92. *Waterford Standard*, Saturday, 16 August 1947, p. 4.
93. *Waterford Standard*, Saturday, 27 August 1949, p. 3.
94. Walton, J. & O'Donoghue, F., *On This Day*, Vol. II.

CHAPTER 21

95. See for example *Liverpool Echo*, Monday, 14 November 1955, p. 7.
96. *Northern Whig*, Saturday, 13 July 1957, p. 2.
97. *Belfast Telegraph*, Friday, 23 March 1956, p. 10.

CHAPTER 22

98. 'Port of Waterford: Extracts from the Records of the Waterford Harbour Commissioners from their Establishment in 1816 to the Reports of the Ports and Harbours Tribunal 1930', Anthony J. Brophy, *Decies*, No. 60, 2004, *JWA&HS*.
99. *Waterford Standard*, Wednesday, 12 February 1896, p. 4.
100. *Greenock Telegraph and Clyde Shipping Gazette*, Thursday, 25 July 1907. p. 2.
101. *Waterford Mirror and Tramore Visitor*, Thursday, 22 August 1907, p. 3.
102. *Waterford Chronicle*, Wednesday, 18 September 1907, p. 3.
103. A bold claim indeed, but one that proved to be correct.
104. Friel was the Waterford harbour engineer. He started in this position in 1898 and served for sixty-five years.
105. *Munster Express*, Saturday, 14 September 1907, p. 5.
106. 'The SS Portlairge', Sonny Condon, *Decies*, No. 63, *JWA&HS*, 2007.
107. Email correspondence with Paul Jacques.
108. *Waterford Standard*, Saturday, 4 July 1953, p. 3.
109. *Irish Independent*, Wednesday, 17 November 1954, p. 4.
110. *Kilkenny People*, Friday, 18 March 1983, p. 9.
111. *Irish Examiner*, Saturday, 14 June 1980, p. 2.
112. *Kilkenny People*, Friday, 9 March 1984, p. 4.
113. Tuesday, 2 December 1986, p. 10.
114. *Irish Examiner*, Thursday, 27 August 1987, p. 5.

CHAPTER 23

115. O'Sullivan, T.F., *Goodly Barrow: A Voyage on an Irish River*, 2001, Lilliput Press, Dublin.
116. A simple web search of the title reveals several online texts.

Bibliography

A Dictionary of the World's Watercraft, The Mariners' Museum, 2000, Chatham Publishing.

A Maritime History of Ringsend, 2000, Sandymount Community Services.

Antell, R., *The Mails Between South West Wales and Southern Ireland: The Milford–Waterford Packet 1600–1850*, 2011, Welsh Philatelic Society.

Babb, A., *U-Boat Enigmas*, 2019, Amazon, UK.

Brophy, A.J., 'Port of Waterford. Extracts from the Records of the Waterford Harbour Commissioners from their Establishment in 1816 to the Report of the Ports and Harbours Tribunal 1930'. *Decies*, No. 60, *Journal of the Waterford Archaeological & Historical Society*, 2004, pp. 151–169.

Colfer, B., *The Hook Peninsula*, 2004, Cork University Press, Cork.

Condon, S., 'The SS Portlairge'. *Decies*, No. 63, *Journal of the Waterford Archaeological & Historical Society*, 2007, pp. 185–192.

Cummins, Patrick J., *Emergency Air Incidents South East Ireland 1940–1945*, 2004, Aviation History Ireland, Waterford.

de Courcy Ireland, J., *Ireland's Sea Fisheries: A History*, 1981, The Glendale Press, Dublin.

Fewer, T.N. (ed.), *I Was a Day in Waterford*, 2001, Ballylough Books, Waterford.

Hutchinson, J.R., *The Press Gang Afloat and Ashore*, 2010, Fireship Press.

Irish, B., 'Waterford Steamship Company'. *Decies*, No. 53, *Journal of the Waterford Archaeological & Historical Society*, 1997, pp. 67–89.

Macintyre, D., *Fighting Under the Sea*, 1965, Evan Brothers Ltd, London.

Maddock, F., *The Cot Fishermen of the River Nore* (eds Nolan, W. & Whelan, K.), Kilkenny History and Society. 1990, Geography Press, pp. 541–565.

McElwee, R., *The Last Voyages of the Waterford Steamers*, 1992, The Book Centre, Waterford.

McRonald, M., *The Irish Boats. Vol. 2. Liverpool to Cork and Waterford*, 2006, Tempus, Stroud, Gloucestershire.

McShane, M., *Neutral Shores. Ireland and the battle of the Atlantic*, 2012, Mercier Press, Cork.

Nolan, L. & J. E., *Secret Victory. Ireland and the War at Sea 1914–18*, 2009, Mercier Press, Cork.

O'Byrne, M., 'Jogging My Memory, The Monks School New Ross in the 1880s'. From *The Past: The Organ of the Uí Cinsealaigh Historical Society*. No. 18, 1992, pp. 55–74.

O'Sullivan, T.F., *Goodly Barrow, A Voyage on an Irish River*, 2001, Lilliput Press, Dublin.

Power, J., *A Maritime History of County Wexford Vol. 1. 1859–1910*, 2011, Olinda Publications, Kilmore Quay, Wexford.

Roberts, B., 'To earn a living under sail', *Yacht and Yachting Magazine*, 11 December 1964.

Roche, R., *Tales of the Wexford Coast*, 1993, Duffry Press, Enniscorthy.

Shepherd, E., *Fishguard & Rosslare Railways & Harbour Company*, 2015, Colourpoint Books, Newtownards.

Smith, G., *King's Cutters. The Revenue Service and the War against Smuggling*, 1983, Conway Maritime Press, London.

Stokes, R., *Between the Tides: Shipwrecks of the Irish Coast*, 2015, Amberley, Gloucestershire.

Walsh, J. (ed.), *Sliabh Rua: A History of its People and Places*, 2001.

Walton, J. & O'Donoghue, F., *On This Day* Vol. II, 2014.

Young, A., *A Tour in Ireland 1776–1779*, 1970, Irish University Press, Shannon.

EARLIER BOOK BY THE AUTHOR

Before the Tide Went Out By Andrew Doherty

Andrew vividly brings you into the heart of a now practically vanished fishing community, deep into the domestic lives of the people making a hard and precarious living from the river, just 6 miles from Waterford city centre. You share his affectionate memories of the local people and the fun that was to be had as a child playing in and around the fishing boats and nets on a busy quayside.

He also takes you out on the river, on bright and beautiful days, and on wild and dangerous nights, which he describes with a natural storytelling turn of phrase. You feel the cold, the misery of sea-soaked clothing and the pain of raw hands hauling on fish-scaled nets.

But what keeps you going is what kept him going for fifteen years, the camaraderie and pride of spending time with brave, skilled and wise fishermen who could be grumpy, hilarious, sometimes eccentric, but never boring.

The destination for history
www.thehistorypress.co.uk